THE COLONIAL ORIGINS
OF THE UNITED STATES: 1607–1763

AMERICAN REPUBLIC SERIES

EDITED BY DON E. FEHRENBACHER AND OTIS A. PEASE

THE COLONIAL ORIGINS OF THE UNITED STATES: 1607-1763

W. W. ABBOT
University of Virginia

John Wiley & Sons, Inc.

NEW YORK • LONDON • SYDNEY • TORONTO

33913-13

Library of Congress Cataloging in Publication Data:

Abbot, William W.   1922–
The colonial origins of the United States, 1607–1763.

(American Republic series)
1.   United States—History—Colonial period, ca. 1660–1775. 2.   Massachusetts—
History—Colonial period, ca. 1660–1775. 3.   Virginia—History—Colonial period, ca.
1660–1775. I.   Title.

E188.A23   973.2   74-28127
ISBN 0-471-00139-2
ISBN 0-471-00140-6 pbk.

Printed in the United States of America

10 9 8 7 6 5

For EPA

Preface

When George Washington delivered his Farewell Address in September, 1796, he stood closer in time to us than he did to the founding of Jamestown. It is easy to forget how much American history took place before the existence of the office of the President. In general histories of the United States, the long line of colonial development is now usually telescoped into a few summary chapters in which the sense of time's passage and of long and complex social growth is likely to be sacrificed. Yet many aspects of modern America cannot be understood until their origins are traced back into the colonial period. The common law, representative government, the spirit of capitalism, and black-white relations are but a few obvious examples. Only scholars specializing in early American history are now disposed to study each of the thirteen colonies in all the detail of their individual foundings and developments. The general reader is likely to prefer a brief account that explains the main themes of the colonial era and catches its spirit and essence, using factual data to illustrate and illuminate. This is the kind of thoughtful compression that W. W. Abbot has achieved in THE COLONIAL ORIGINS OF THE UNITED STATES, 1607–1763. He has made a virtue of the need to be selective and brief in the treatment of one and one-half centuries. His book is chronologically the first volume in the "Wiley American Republic Series," a joint effort at exploring the meaning of the past to the present in separate volumes written by specialists in the fields.

Don Fehrenbacher
Otis Pease

Contents

Chapter I

Introduction

Europe was on the move in the sixteenth century. Not since the days of the first Caesar had there been such a reaching out and taking in by Europeans. All at once new worlds became known and old worlds became accessible. Because they were there and known to be there, and because Europe and Europeans were what they were and were becoming, these worlds, early or late, got to be the business of one or another of the European powers, to be subjugated or peopled, exploited or developed, Christianized and civilized—in short, to be dominated for their own good and the good of their souls and for the power and glory, and enrichment, of their European masters. Over the span of four centuries Europeans managed much of the earth and did it with a seemingly irresistible drive to remake all men in their own image. It was as unlikely and important a business as men have ever engaged in.

European dominance has drawn together these new and old worlds of Columbus's day into the one world of the twentieth century. If the Europeans in the end failed to make little brothers of the Asians and Africans, or even faithful sons of the transplanted Europeans in the Americas, they succeeded only too well in instilling the lessons they themselves gradually learned to live by, that a people is itself the best judge of its own good and that every man, given even a modicum of freedom, stands some chance of enjoying the sweets of the here and now. These urges toward nationhood and individual advancement, taught by Western example and given

1

force and direction by Western techniques and technology, led ultimately to the general destruction of the crasser form of European domination by outright political control. Having sowed and cultivated the seeds of its own destruction, European expansionism may take what comfort it can from the spectacle of a contracted Europe living in a world Europeanizing itself with dizzying rapidity.

The first peoples to destroy the dominion of their European mother country and establish independent nationhood were neither alien nor subjugated. The English colonists of continental North America were transplanted Europeans sharing with Europe its essential view of man and his society and, on the eve of their revolution, enjoying perhaps a wider area of individual freedom and opportunity than their counterparts in Britain itself. Having brought with them and nurtured European patterns of life and thought, they did not have to develop European aspirations or adopt European assumptions about themselves and their lives before being brought to the point of revolt. The sturdy growth of this transplant had after a century and a half produced a society European in origin and in character but sufficiently distinct and independent to find in itself both the impulse and the capacity to sever the political bonds that tied it to the Old World.

For the American considering the American past, the road from Jamestown to Lexington and Concord is a winding one full of chance and mischance. The Revolution that followed he finds endlessly fascinating and its outcome something to marvel at. The African revolutionist of the second half of the twentieth century would not have the same view of the United States's colonial period and its revolution. For the Asian or the African whose success in rejecting the West and Western control has been predicated on his ability simultaneously to westernize his land and people, the American road to revolution must seem inexplicably long and its success somewhat less than marvelous. Whatever the lesson it does or does not teach to emerging nations, however, the story of the Americanization of the European settlers on the Atlantic coast of North America, of which the Revolution was only the product and the fulfillment, is interesting in itself and instructive.

One way to get at this American story is to view it as a chapter

in the expansion of the West. As such, it is a part of the story of
Britain's projecting herself into the New World. The dynamics of
the piece becomes the progressive development of British imperial
connections that finally snap in 1776, only to be replaced on this
side of the water in 1789 by a similar, though now American and
not British, engine of government. The tendency of those who so
view the emergence of the United States is to place their emphasis
on the survival of English and European traits in the American
character, to find evidence everywhere of the persistence of the
English heritage and of America's unlimited indebtedness to English institutions. Early American history becomes in a sense the saga
of the Europeanization of America.

Others who take a different view of early America choose to
search for and trace out not what survived the sea change and
withstood the grinding impact of the American land and climate,
but rather what of the old was changed, however subtly, and what
was newly introduced into the life and character of these people as
a consequence of their radically altered circumstances. After all, the
things that are distinctive about Americans are the best clues to
what Americans are and what the United States is. And certainly
much that is distinctively American derives from the experience of
Americans as colonials for a century and a half on the rim of a vast
and virtually empty continent, far from the centers of Europe. This
being so, something other than the development of imperial relations between Britain and her colonies is needed to hang the tale
on. The really important thing that happened in America before the
Revolution, it would seem, is that a new and different society, one
akin to Europe but not European, emerged and established itself.
This then, the evolution of a new society, becomes the proper story
line for early American history.

The real difference between these two approaches to the colonial
past, often blurred, becomes most distinct when the story reaches
its finale in the American Revolution. If the story up to 1763 has
been told largely in terms of the development of political and
economic relationships within the British Empire, its climactic chapter in the American Revolution finds at the root of the crisis in
imperial relations a misuse of power and its faulty distribution
among the component parts of the empire. The Revolution itself

represents a failure to resolve this crisis, and the Federal Constitution its resolution by a workable redistribution and limitation of power in the new American empire or union. If, on the other hand, the story has been mainly that of the emergence of a new society distinctively American, the crisis in the empire leading to the Revolution is taken as evidence that the new American society could no longer be contained in the old imperial mold, that the British connection had come to distort this society and to inhibit its natural development. The break with Britain, therefore, represents the removal of one inhibition upon this society's realizing itself, which, so it goes, it is still in the process of doing.

Any investigator of the American past who focuses on the development of the colonies as components of the British Empire has the advantage of a readymade plot for his tale. By concentrating on Britain's colonial policy and its effect on thirteen of her colonies, he has not only a progression of events he can follow in time but also a convenient vantage point from which to view these varied and disconnected colonies—an important consideration when it is remembered that before the 1760s the only consistently tangible connections between, say, Savannah, Georgia, and Portsmouth, New Hampshire, ran through the offices at Whitehall in London. The person taking this approach is also more likely to grasp the significance of the undeniable but often not fully appreciated fact that for the first half of its history what is now the United States was part and parcel of Europe's political and economic systems. The shifts of fortune among the great powers of Europe time and again spelled prosperity or ruin for a Virginia tobacco planter, life or death for the inhabitants of a New Hampshire village. In terms of its involvement in the world at large, America of the twentieth century is much closer to the seventeenth and eighteenth centuries than to the nineteenth. And, finally, an emphasis on America's English heritage makes for a more balanced if less precisely detailed picture of the colonial American and his America than does the search for the unique and distinctive in colonial life. It is, for instance, easy to forget that behind the Americanization of Anglican church government in Virginia or of English Puritanism in Massachusetts there rises that mountain of truth that the Old World passed Christianity on to America; and, as important as it is that the land and forests of America blurred English class distinctions, it is perhaps more important that American settlers retained the European family structure.

The trouble is that this "imperial" approach to early American history is likely to reveal more about the workings of the old empire or about America's debt to the Old World than most students of America's past either wish or perhaps need to know. What they do wish and need to know is who they are and how they got that way. Part of the answer lies in an understanding of the society that emerged in America and at the end of the eighteenth century assumed its independent political existence. The non-Westerner considering for the first time eighteenth-century Europe and America would be hard put to distinguish between the mental make-up of the two; but the nearer one draws to America and Britain the more apparent the differences become, and from the vantage point of London or of Chicago many of the characteristics shared by Britain and her colonies begin to fade into the obvious, to become things that go without saying. The differences, now brought into high relief, become the marks of national identity. Although the American in search of his national identity will find no single complete and coherent statement of just how the miscellaneous European immigrants who settled between Maine and Georgia became the Americans of 1776, or even of precisely what the Americans of 1776 were, there is a vast body of evidence to permit him to form his own views of the matter.

No historian, of course, has followed either approach to the exclusion of the other. Anyone seeking to discover how the trade of the colonies fitted into Britain's economy, or why the governors in royal colonies tended after about 1720 to lose ground steadily to the lower houses of the legislature, will certainly see the relevance to his investigation of the emergence in America of distinctive social patterns and attitudes. If, on the other hand, it is these distinctive patterns and attitudes he is after, he will hardly have to be told that imperial institutions and the fact of continuing British supervision did much to determine how colonial Americans lived, learned, made their way, moved about and multiplied, worshiped, and saw themselves and the world about them. The choice made here to seek for clues to social realities of our national origins by telling how familiar institutions got started, altered, and became fixed has at least one thing in its favor: it forces us to begin at the beginning and to move forward in time to some sort of an end.

Chapter II

England Reaches Out

Before England really got around to doing anything about the New World the Spanish empire was a century old. By then, the silver and other riches the Spaniards funneled into Europe from America had transformed Europe—and England with it. Late in the sixteenth century a combination of circumstances, some of them centuries in the making, permitted the English to launch their bid for an overseas empire. During the reign of Elizabeth I, England found herself for the first time with the means and the opportunity, and with the consequent urge, to compete with the continental powers for a share of the New World. During the next half century she spawned English America. The circumstance of the mother country at the time of English America's birth put its mark upon the child. It also set for the future certain patterns of relationship between England and her colonies, patterns that did much to define the British Empire as it took shape during the next century.

By the time Elizabeth came to the throne in 1558, England's wealth was becoming great enough to make ventures on the scale of colonization possible. This new-found wealth was based ultimately on a long-term revolution in agriculture. When in the eleventh and twelfth centuries there had occurred a general revival of commerce in Europe, particularly in Italy, the towns of northern Germany, the Lowlands, and in northern France, England had been a land remote from the center of activity, bound largely to subsistence farming on the medieval manor. The economic revival of

Europe sharply increased the demand for cloth. Cloth meant woolens; and, as it happened, England was peculiarly suited to sheep raising. The long process of enclosing and converting into pasture land the fields cultivated by manorial serfs began. Partly as a consequence, there developed in England a chronic oversupply of labor and a shortage of food. The sale of wool to Europe was at the same time creating a money economy in England. Merchants were accumulating from the sale of wool abroad surplus capital for investment; former serfs were becoming independent peasants selling their surplus crops for cash at advancing prices; and large landholders were raising sheep with hired workers and selling the wool to English merchants.

Increasing wealth and increasing opportunity to acquire it in turn hastened the process by which the men of England were eventually brought to the point where they could and indeed must reach out across the sea for colonies. All the ingredients required to make England a competitor instead of a dependent hinterland of the more advanced states of Europe were present well before the opening of the sixteenth century: raw wool in large quantity; a great market for woolen cloth; surplus capital amassed by merchants in the wool trade; and a large, cheap, and mobile labor supply. Acquisitive Englishmen who had first become wool merchants now became entrepreneurs who, instead of selling the wool they bought from the sheep growers, hired the labor to make it into cloth and sold the cloth in both domestic and foreign markets. Markets for cloth were, of course, far less restricted than for wool, and profits from its sale far greater. By Elizabeth's day these merchant-capitalists had not only broken the stranglehold of foreigners on England's coastwise and overseas shipping but they had in fact also established England's management of her foreign trade. In so doing, they had become the most dynamic if not the most conspicuous and powerful segment of English society. It was they who were to provide the thrust for the first successful overseas expansion of England, the machinery for organizing it, the money for carrying it out, and the determination required to sustain it. Without the ships and seamen called into being by foreign trade, colonization could not even have been attempted. Without the capital accumulated by the traders, colonization could not, or would not, have been sufficiently supported. Without the experience of organizing and conducting large and risky trading ventures, the pooling of resources required for successful colonization could have been accomplished only by the state, which Elizabeth and her successors consistently refused to permit. And without the examples of wealth being accumulated in trade and the hunger for wealth this engendered, Englishmen would hardly have been willing to pay the price in lives, toil, and treasure that colonization ultimately exacted.

But the merchant-capitalists not only made colonization possible and probable; as chief colonizers they were also in time to do much to fix the nature and function of the colonies. Had the first English settlement in America yielded a repetition of the Spanish bonanza, as was hoped, support for colonization would have been no problem and what was strictly mercantile in its character would undoubtedly have been diluted. It turned out, however, that only trade could make the first colony worth the expense and bother, and much of the Virginia social and institutional pattern derives from the merchant-colonizers' efforts to make the colony a producer of crops for the English market and a consumer of goods the English had to sell.

If, instead of merchants, courtiers and the landed great of England had engineered the first successful colonization, it is hard to believe—and we are not without evidence on this—that they would have been so eager to send out English settlers to Virginia in such numbers, that they would have so quickly adopted a public land policy based on the capacity of the potential owner to make it productive, that they would have been so ready to share control of the enterprise with the planters, or that they would have been so concerned with following English legal procedure in Virginia. This is not to say that had English colonization come without the intervention of the merchants, settlement by Englishmen on a large scale, private and widespread ownership of land, representative government, and the rule of law would have been forever withheld, for they probably would not. Witness Massachusetts. But it is to say that it was important that this mercantile impulse, which can be seen operating as late as 1732 in the founding of Georgia, did so much to give initial form to a colonial prototype in Virginia.

Certainly there can be no denying that the British imperial structure as it took shape during the seventeenth century was mercantile in character, designed and maintained to serve English trade. All of the European colonizing powers measured the worth of a colony in terms of its value to the mother country, but its value could be measured in several ways: to the extent it offered landed estates and wealth to the nation's ruling aristocracy; in the amount of gold and silver it poured into the king's treasury; by the prestige and more particularly the strategic advantage it gave the state. But the importance to Britain of foreign trade and the influence this gave to the merchants who conducted it assured that a colony's worth to England would in the last analysis be judged by how profitable it was for the English merchants to peddle English goods in the colony and buy native products from it. It should be noted that Massachusetts and her New England offshoots sprang from a different impulse in English life, one that was transitory and may be called accidental or providential. New England took on life largely independent of the mercantile ideal as conceived by the English merchants, and it was not easily, or in a sense ever really, accommodated to the mercantile empire, not even when for a time in the eighteenth century the empire seemed to fulfill its rationale that what was good for the whole was good for its parts, that English profits assured colonial prosperity and well-being.

And so it appears that developments in foreign trade in sixteenth-century England not only made future colonizing ventures possible, and likely, but also did much to predetermine what the colonies and empire would be when colonization did come. But Britain's great empire of the eighteenth century was still far in the future when Elizabeth came to the throne of England in 1558; and an empire is not made simply of a growing capacity to colonize and a quickening impulse to do so. England for the moment was barred from conquering new worlds by her precarious position in the old one. The political situation in Europe was exceedingly unstable. Earlier in the century Martin Luther had entered the wedge that split Christendom. By 1558 Europe was divided into two hostile camps, one Protestant and the other Roman Catholic, each with a mandate from God to prevail. A sixteenth-century Christian, whether Catholic or Protestant, could as well accept the fact that the One God was Two as accept the possibility of His having two true churches.

Protestant and Catholic were each convinced that the other had to be made to see the light or be destroyed. By the same token, no European ruler could imagine ruling without the support of a unified church. Either he was able to enforce adherence to the religion of the state or he demonstrated his incapacity to govern. It took a century of bloodletting to force people here and there to accept the necessity of the unthinkable—religious toleration. Their rulers were generally even longer in conceding the possibility of separating church and state. Neither of these modern concepts, incidentally, was among the notions the Puritans brought to Massachusetts.

The countries whose people remained all Catholic or became all Protestant were by and large spared the horrifying storms stirred up in other parts of Europe by religious controversy. The Spanish, the Portuguese, and the people of the Italian city-states stuck with the Mother Church; the Scandinavian peoples and the Scots went over to Protestantism. But the Germans, the French, the people of the Spanish Lowlands, and the English were not all one or the other. It was in these places that the trouble came.

Germany was first to be racked with religious strife. By the time of Elizabeth's accession in 1558 the first chapter in the sad tale of Germany's religious troubles was already finished. After almost a lifetime of struggle to suppress the Lutheran heresy, Emperor Charles V in 1555 had reluctantly settled for a Germany of small states, each either Catholic or Protestant according to the decision of its petty ruler. The fragmentation of Germany, which was confirmed and carried to completion in the Thirty Years' War of the next century, among other things eliminated Germany as a possible competitor of the Atlantic seaboard powers in the colonization of America. Neighboring France, for her part, predominantly Catholic under a Catholic king but with an influential Protestant minority, was by 1558 ripening for internal strife. In the Spanish Lowlands to the north, the growth of a Protestant movement was inviting Spanish intervention. England's situation at Elizabeth's accession, equally fraught with danger, was peculiar.

Elizabeth's father, Henry VIII, had taken the English church out of the Universal Church by rejecting the Pope, and had stripped it of much of its independent wealth and power, but he had not made it Protestant. Under his son, Edward VI, the English church had veered sharply toward Protestantism only to be re-Catholicized briefly by Mary, his successor. When Elizabeth became Queen, she quickly showed herself not the sort of ruler who would concede control of the church either to the Pope or to Protestant preachers. Her decision to reconfirm the English church's independence of Rome was bolstered by her knowledge that in the eyes of the Papacy she was an illegitimate child of Henry without right to succeed to the throne. At the same time, her determination not to surrender control of the state church to the strongly Protestant subjects who were pressing her became forever fixed by the necessity that she avoid alienating her subjects whose leanings were less Protestant or not at all so. Her solution for the Anglican church, known popularly as the Elizabethan Settlement, served to put off England's religious war for three quarters of a century, and it opened the way for Elizabeth to foster the national unity that England had to have if she were ever to challenge the dominance of Spain and plant colonies in America. The more ardent English Protestants continued to hope that they would eventually rid Elizabeth's church of its Romish impurities. Not until long after her death did large numbers despair of achieving this in England. It was then that several thousand of them went out to Massachusetts.

Lack of national unity and stability was but one of the barriers to England's overseas expansion in the early years of Elizabeth's reign. The two great Catholic powers, France and Spain, threatened Elizabeth's throne and ultimately even the economic and political independence of England itself. France had at hand in the person of Mary Stuart, Queen of the Scots and from 1559 to 1560 Queen of France, its candidate to replace the usurper Elizabeth. Once she should become Queen of the English, Mary would be able to bring England back into the Roman Church and under the influence of her archenemy France. King Philip of Spain, as the leader of the forces dedicated to re-Catholicizing Europe, was even more anxious to snatch England from the Protestant clutches of Elizabeth, but he was hardly enthusiastic about replacing her with French-dominated Mary. Dependent upon trade with Spain and wishing to forestall Philip's joining forces with France on Mary's behalf, Elizabeth paid court to the Spanish King, who was nothing loath, for he feared a union of French and English seapower if Mary should succeed to the English throne. It was during this stage of Anglo-Spanish relations, in the first decade of Elizabeth's reign, that Elizabeth sanctioned and Spain tolerated John Hawkins' illicit and highly profitable trade in African slaves with the Spanish colonists in the West Indies. In 1568, Mary fled her Protestant subjects in Scotland and took refuge with her cousin Elizabeth. Shortly thereafter war flared up between Catholic and Protestant forces in France, effectively removing France from the European equation for nearly a generation. The situation had changed drastically. Now Spain alone stood between Elizabethan England and her proper place in the sun.

The rapidly intensifying rivalry between England and Spain strengthened the English impulse to claim a portion of the New World, and the climax to the rivalry which came in the defeat of Spain's armada in 1588 opened the way for successful English colonization in 1607. England's reliance upon trade with Spain to provide markets for her staple, woolen cloth, and the dyestuffs to color it with, reinforced Elizabeth's caution in dealing with Philip. It at the same time made clearer the urgency of England's challenging Spain in the New World. Only by establishing colonies in America could she be certain of lessening this dangerous dependency upon her most powerful rival. The savage destruction of Hawkins' fleet at San Juan de Ulloa in 1568 had ended any hopes of a peaceful penetration of the Spanish Empire in America. Anti-Spanish feeling aroused by the treatment of Hawkins was kept alive and intensified during the next twenty years by Spanish intrigue to replace Elizabeth on the throne with Mary, who became a suitable instrument of Spanish policy after her flight from Scotland and upon the eruption of civil conflict in France. Although Elizabeth held back from a complete break with Spain until 1586 when she forced the issue by permitting the execution of Mary, she kept raising the pressure after 1568, first by unleashing her "sea dogs" like Francis Drake to prey on Spanish shipping and then by giving material aid to the Dutch Protestants across the Channel in their fight for independence from Spain.

The stepped-up activity of the English in American waters was both a cause and a consequence of the growing antagonism between England and Spain. Except for those lured by the prospects of Spanish plunder, however, English seamen in the 1570s seemed at first to be drawn to America only to find their way around it. On one voyage, Drake sailed south and through the Strait of Magellan to seek the rich continent believed to be awaiting discovery in the South Pacific beyond, while Frobisher kept to the north in search of a northwest passage to the Orient, the best remedy for Portugal's monopoly of the trade with the East. And others followed where Drake and Frobisher had led.

Near the end of the decade interest began to shift from eastern voyages and to focus on the potentialities of the North American continent itself. After Sir Humphrey Gilbert was lost at sea in a colonizing venture in 1582, his half-brother Sir Walter Raleigh mounted an expedition which planted a colony on Roanoke Sound in 1585. Although Drake brought the settlers away before fresh supplies could arrive, Thomas Hariot's report on the venture, printed first in 1588, and again in 1590 with engravings of John White's fine water colors of American flora and fauna, served to widen interest in this strange land. Raleigh's second colony on the Carolina coast, planted in 1587, had disappeared when Governor White finally returned with supplies in 1590 after the defeat of the Armada. And so ended colonizing by Elizabethan courtiers. But England had turned her attention to colonization, the attempt had been made, and much had been learned. The question remained whether the fruits of all this could be harvested, and how soon.

The man most responsible for keeping the vision of colonies alive from the time of Raleigh's lost colony in 1590 to the founding of the Virginia Company in 1606 was the same man who with his older cousin, both named Richard Hakluyt, had done more than any others to create the vision in the first place. Their writings had aroused and sustained interest in colonization in the late 1570s and through the 1580s; but their supreme achievement had been to project colonization in terms of broad national interests, to make clear what the purposes of colonization properly were and what functions colonies could be realistically expected to serve. Implanted firmly in the English mind by the end of the century was the idea that the good of the nation demanded that colonies be established and that they be established in a way to serve that good.

What the Hakluyts had in fact accomplished was to harness colonization to the exulting national pride and vaulting national ambition
of Elizabethan England.

To make her bid for greatness, England required colonies in
North America. She required them, as the Hakluyts helped make
people understand, to secure products that only her enemies could
supply, to their gain and England's loss; to develop markets for
England's woolens and other goods and thereby provide work for
her unemployed, profit for her merchants, income for the Queen's
treasury, and prosperity for the whole; to weaken the power of
Spain and assure the national safety by serving as strategic bases
near the shipping lanes of the western Atlantic; to increase the
number of "stronge shippes and able mariners" for protection of
the island nation in time of peril; and to serve God and secure His
blessings by converting the heathen. And if stores of precious metal
were found to enrich the nation, so much the better. But at bottom
the Hakluyts were demanding that the colonies be producers and
consumers—producers of those products England was without and
needed; consumers of those goods that England made, could make
in ever larger quantities, and must sell.

Although the arguments of the Hakluyts were initially directed
mainly toward the courtier-colonizers and their Queen, who were
apt to think more in terms of gold and silver and landed wealth than
in terms of trade, their program of colonization fitted exactly the
aspirations of the great merchants who until after the turn of the
century were directing their energies and resources to opening up
trade to the eastward. When the merchants in the seaports, London
in particular, finally did turn their attention to the west, to America,
they found a blueprint for action ready at hand, and they proceeded
to demonstrate their unique capacity to make the Hakluyt vision of
colonies a reality.

At the opening of the seventeenth century, the English were
alive to the possibilities of the New World and had some experience in it. They had met Spain on her own terms and had prevailed.
Their island kingdom lying off the coast of Europe in the Atlantic,
which had replaced the Mediterranean as the highway of the world,
provided a superb base from which to launch and protect overseas
ventures. Their economy demanded that they expand beyond the

limits of their island and would support the cost of that expansion. And they were bursting with energy and with confidence that they were a people marked for greatness. The road to empire lay open, and England was ready for the journey.

On April 10, 1606, James I issued to the Virginia Company of London and of Plymouth and the outports a charter authorizing the two groups of "adventurers" to begin colonies on the Atlantic seaboard of America between the thirty-fourth and forty-first degrees north latitude. Ten months later, the first contingent of English settlers set sail for the coast of North America.

Chapter III

The Beginnings: Virginia

The great migration of English folk began in 1607. Before the flow dropped to a trickle after 1640, many thousands of men, women, and children of all sorts and conditions had come out and settled on the banks of the rivers of the Chesapeake, the islands of the West Indies, and along the coast and into the interior of New England. Why, we ask, did these people pick up and go across the sea to undertake the difficult and dangerous business of planting nations in the wilderness?

Why men do what they do at any given time and place is a mystery students of the past forever probe and never finally penetrate. The motives prompting a man to go to Virginia in 1609, or to Massachusetts in 1630, were likely as complex as the man himself, and no two men were the same. But certain broad motives widely shared by those who settled in Virginia before 1630 are discernible, just as they are for those who later went to New England. Like the "knights, gentlemen, merchants" and ordinary people who put up the money for the venture, settlers going out to Virginia went as patriots, as Christians, and as men seeking personal profit, the betterment of their lot: "for the good of your country and your own, and to serve and fear God the giver of all goodness," as His Majesty's Council put it in its instructions to the first settlers. The thing that continued to draw them after all else seemed to fail, however, was land. The immense forests, valuable in themselves, were always waiting to be made into fields for raising crops—

for the good of their country and their own.

But this is to beg the question. Why did this man go and that one stay? Why did the prospect of owning land lure this land-hungry farmer and not that one? Why did one man, his ambitions foiled, try again in the New World and another learn to live with his disappointments? Why did some flee tyrannical fathers, shrewish mothers-in-law, demanding mistresses, or simply the "displeasuer" of friends and neighbors, while others remained to endure what was to be endured? Or, for that matter, why, later, did a devout Puritan choose the new Zion of Massachusetts and the equally devout parishioner in the neighboring pew decide to stick with what they both feared to be hopelessly corrupted?

Most could not have explained had they wished, and few tried. What is obvious, though, is that from the start the challenge of America imposed a sort of selective process upon emigration. For good or ill, America began by attracting those Englishmen with a temperament, a kind of personality bias, that pushed them into reaching for the unknown, whether to escape what they had come to consider intolerable or, perhaps more likely, to seek what they held to be desirable: attention from their fellows, land, employment, advanced station, adventure, self-justification, eternal salvation, or what have you. Before the American environment could well begin its work, Americans as a people were already active, not passive; aggressive, not timid; mobile, not fixed; ambitious, not self-satisfied; restless, adventurous, energetic, optimistic: their being where they were was evidence enough of all this. To argue that it may too have been evidence of an individual's irresponsibility, instability, callousness, shiftlessness, selfishness, a taste for violence, or still worse things only reinforces the point that certain tendencies of the American character were perhaps being culled even as men boarded ships in the Thames for passage to Jamestown.

The first group to sail for Virginia was sent out in late December 1606 by the London "adventurers" of the recently chartered Virginia Company. The men in this advance party were to look over the land and to establish a base for future operations. Once they had chosen a site suitable for settlement and provided for its protection, they were to get down to the main business at hand—a search for minerals, particularly gold, silver, and copper, and for rivers that flowed into "the East India Sea." The discovery of either would assure the immediate success of the venture. They were also to persuade the Indians to concede the right of trade and to convey sufficient land for planting in return for the manifest blessings of Christianity and civilization which the English presence would impart. Once he had been "civilized" by the European, the Indian would of course become an eager customer for English goods. This bargain, incidentally, was one that the white man was to offer the North American natives again and again through the centuries. The Indians did not buy it at Jamestown nor did they buy it thereafter. In the meantime, as they were making their arrangements with the Indians, the settlers would plant gardens for their sustenance and put up houses for their shelter, laying the foundations for the gradual buildup of a flourishing English settlement in Virginia.

Only a few of the hundred-odd who went out—gentlemen, artisans, a clergyman, a surgeon, soldiers, a sailor, and several boys—survived the first summer and winter in Virginia. Even so, by the spring of 1608 Englishmen had succeeded in establishing an outpost on a peninsula in the James River which was easily accessible yet could be defended from attack from land or sea by relatively few men. In the summer of 1608, Captain John Smith explored the shores of the bay from which the colonists had sailed into the James. He discovered no gold or silver mines and no water passage to the Pacific. What he did find was in the long run perhaps as important. He found that the Chesapeake, with its entrance conveniently narrowed at the mouth by two capes, was an enormous bay fed by magnificent rivers providing easy access to the interior on every side. Down to the Revolution the bay with its rivers, the James, the York, the Rappahannock, the Potomac, the Susquehanna, the Patuxent, and the Severn, would serve as the lifeline of the Chesapeake colonies, holding them together as they expanded while providing them with convenient means of traffic with the outside world. On his return to Jamestown from his explorations, Smith assumed control of the quarreling little settlement and, aided by supplies and reinforcements from England, carried it through its second year.

By the end of 1608 the London managers of the venture had concluded that a new approach to the problem of colonizing Virginia was necessary. Clearly, neither gold nor a northwest passage was going to provide a quick solution, whatever the future prospects; and to continue the policy of sending settlers out "little by little" was clearly to settle for a draw in the battle with the hostile American environment. The little colony was only barely maintaining its toehold on the banks of the James. What was immediately required, it now appeared, was a sufficient number of settlers to clear considerably more land and get it into production. This alone would assure the colony's survival, get it onto its own feet and set it into motion. The London adventurers had until now managed the venture under the authority of the charter granted by the King to the Virginia Company in 1606; but recognizing that to send out and supply large numbers of settlers required a great deal of money, they opened their books in February 1609 to public subscription to a joint-stock fund. At the same time they applied to the King for a new charter reorganizing the company, with all those subscribing to the joint stock to be listed as adventurers. Their plan was to have 600 new settlers in Virginia by early summer and nearly three times that before the summer was over. Time was short enough for engaging ships and purchasing supplies to mount expeditions of such unprecedented size, to say nothing of the necessity of persuading suitable people to go out while inducing others to contribute to the joint-stock fund to pay for it all. What was achieved is astonishing. In early May 1609 a fleet of nine vessels under the command of Sir George Somers set sail for Virginia with about 600 passengers. The feat could have been achieved only by great London merchants like Sir Thomas Smith, who was the guiding spirit of the venture. No other group in England had the combination of experience, resources, and connections to pull it off.

The steps these London merchants took in 1609 to reorganize and promote their company and its colony do much to reveal what Jamestown was all about. The developments of 1609 also suggest why it is useful to pay close attention to the Jamestown story. It is not just that a number of important American patterns and institutions first emerged at Jamestown, for most of these emerge elsewhere largely independent of their prior existence in Virginia. It is rather that the process of planting English colonies repeated many times in the future stands in starkest relief here where it was experienced for the first time, unaffected by the experience of earlier colonies and unsupported by neighboring ones. To understand the Jamestown story is to go far toward understanding the colonization process itself.

In 1609 those promoting the development of the colony in Virginia faced squarely the necessities of the case. Lest all come to naught, a steady supply of money to finance Virginia, and of men to settle it, had to be found. Neither would be forthcoming without the other, and neither the one nor the other would be forthcoming unless people could be persuaded that Virginia had something to offer. Men as a rule do not invest their lives or their fortunes without first being convinced of the likelihood of a good return. The company, then, was under the continuing and compelling necessity in 1609 and afterward of doing everything in its power to render Virginia attractive to both investor and settler. To make the circle of difficulties complete, the adventurers' failure in the first two years to discover anything other than crops raised by English settlers which might provide an economic base for the colony meant, as it turned out, that Virginia could only be made attractive to investors and settlers if investors invested and settlers settled.

The important thing about all this is that the company's search for ways to attract men and money to the Virginia venture largely determined what it did in the colony itself. That is, the shape Virginia took under the direction of the company was in no small measure the consequence of the company's unremitting search for a solution to this problem of supply. (The general relevance of what was operating here becomes clearer when we remember that a century and a half later it was the same problem of supply—though this time the need was for men as soldiers, not settlers, as well as for money—that led Britain to adopt a series of measures that alienated her American colonies and prepared them for revolt.)

The conditions set for the joint stock of 1609 reveal some of the implications for Virginia of the pressures exerted on the London Company by its need for capital and for volunteers to go out to the colony. To get the capital they required, the London adventurers offered membership in the new London Company to anyone who would pay into the joint-stock fund as much as £12 10s. The company was proposing for the next seven years to support the colony from company funds as required and to receive from the colony any surplus income from its operation. To induce people to invest, the company promised each member his share of this expected income. At the end of seven years, in 1616, the joint stock would be terminated and the company would divide its assets, including land in Virginia, between its members in proportion to what each had invested. It would not do to leave it at this, however. Raising funds was only half the problem; the adventurers also had to recruit artisans and energetic planters. To give incentive for settlement, the joint stock included an offer to any man going out to Virginia on his own adventure (that is, at his own expense) what was in effect membership in the company with the equivalent of at least one £12 10s. share when it came to paying dividends and dividing assets.

In using the familiar joint-stock device to pool capital and labor, the Virginia promoters had hit upon a way to channel effectively the long-developing colonizing impulse of the English public and to sustain it through all the bitter disappointments to follow. More than this, they had also—in granting settlers equality of status with English investors—set the future tone, and the future direction, of English colonization. English colonies were not to be simply overseas plantations owned by men in England and worked by servants sent out by English masters; they were to be communities of Englishmen owing allegiance to London but having by right some voice, however minimal, in matters affecting their own welfare. Colonies were also to be undertakings in which Englishmen in large numbers permanently settled a compact area and together pushed back the wilderness on a solid front, not merely entrepôts on the coast manned by employees sent out by English trading companies to conduct their trade with the natives.

If the condition set by the joint stock did not make this last clear, the campaign for subscriptions and settlers in the spring of 1609 did. Although continuing to hold out the prospects of profits from the discovery of precious metals and a northwest passage and from native trade, the promoters put new and greater emphasis on the potential of trade based upon crops raised by English settlers. Already the need for men and money had forced the tacit recognition that land was the company's one tangible and unproblematical asset. How the company used this asset in its persistent struggle to make Virginia attractive to investment and settlement is what gives the rest of the Jamestown story much of its significance.

The charter granted in 1609 to the London adventurers by James I did away with the royal council of the Virginia Company of 1606, which had governed the activities of both the London adventurers, who had planted Jamestown, and the Plymouth adventurers, whose efforts to colonize far up the coast at Sagadahoc had failed, and replaced it with a new council whose authority extended only over the London Company and its enterprises. The council named by the King in the new charter was composed of leading London adventurers—those London merchants who had managed and financed the Jamestown enterprise during its first two years and were now promoting the joint-stock association. The treasurer of the council, Sir Thomas Smith, presided over the company made up of joint-stock subscribers as well as over the council. The treasurer and council had under the charter wide authority to conduct most of the affairs of the company and to provide for the management of the colony. The members of the company could vote to remove the treasurer and councilors from office, but the King appointed these officers and he retained an effective veto over their removal.

The salient features of this arrangement are that the leading adventurers in the Virginia enterprise retained control over both the company in London and the colony in Virginia, and that as "His Majesty's Council" they derived sanction for their control from the King himself. The transfer of sanctions to distant Virginia was a chancy business at best, and the royal authority commanding habitual obedience which the King lent to the council and through it to government in Virginia was of inestimable value. It is easy to forget that there was nothing to guarantee that Englishmen once in America would not reject the irksome restraints required for good order, ultimately reverting perhaps even to a kind of barbarism in that rough land.

The importance of the company's maintaining effective authority in the colony through its agents there—and by inference the importance generally of political institutions to any society—was soon demonstrated. Before Somers sailed with his fleet in May 1609 the council of the London Company, dissatisfied with the council of settlers which had governed the colony with ill success, appointed a resident governor, Lord Delaware, who was to be advised by a council of colonists but bound only by instructions from the company and council in London and by the proviso of the charter guaranteeing colonists the liberties, franchises, and immunities enjoyed by all English subjects. Unfortunately the ship carrying the leaders of the expedition, including Somers and Sir Thomas Gates, was wrecked off Bermuda. The other vessels got to Jamestown near the end of summer, so late in the season that only by strenuous and well-directed efforts could they have erected the shelters and accumulated the provisions needed for the coming winter. Instead, in the absence of duly constituted authority capable of commanding obedience, they fell to bickering and accomplished little or nothing. It was a winter of horror. The next spring, when Somers arrived from Bermuda, he found only sixty settlers still alive; four hundred and more had died during the winter from "famine and pestilence," or at the hands of the Indians. The high hopes and elaborate plans of 1609 had come to this.

In early June, Lieutenant Governor Gates decided to evacuate the remnant; he had abandoned Jamestown and the ships were down the river ready to sail for England when word came that Lord Delaware was in the Bay with supplies and reinforcements. Returning to Jamestown, the colonists set to work under the direction of Delaware. During the summer the Governor sent ships to Bermuda for food and Gates back to England to tell the London Company of the disaster that had befallen their Virginia project.

Upon hearing Gates's distressing report in September 1610, the Virginia council's first impulse was to abandon the venture. It decided to persevere, however. What followed is unmistakable evidence of full recognition by the leading adventurers that their investment in Virginia had proven to be a long-term one that would pay off, if at all, largely in the coin of increased national prosperity, and this only if the company could sufficiently settle Virginia with planters to raise crops for which there was a market in England. Such a view of the colony permitted the adventurers to base their campaign for additional funds to succor Jamestown on a frank appeal to men's patriotism. The effectiveness of the appeal is proof of the pudding, a sign of the wide acceptance of Jamestown as an expression of national purpose deserving public support. Furthermore, the uses to which they put the money they raised—the kind of supplies they accumulated and the sort of settlers they recruited for Virginia in 1611—confirms that the London adventurers had become firmly committed to the goal of developing a colony of planters who would, it was expected, produce such things as wine, sugar, and tropical fruits for the English market. None of this is to say that the Virginia promoters had abandoned all hopes for discoveries that would bring quick and easy profits, but it is clear that by 1611 their fixed intentions were to go ahead with the project without reference to anything except the prospects of utilizing and exploiting the land in Virginia. It is well that they were, for that is all there was.

As a result of the company's efforts in 1611, Jamestown made good progress during the year and even established a second settlement up the river; but, at the end of four years, about all the colony was able to do in the way of fulfilling the company's purposes was to send home an occasional shipment of timber, sassafras, or animal skins got from the Indians. Because of this, the sources of funds for its support were drying up. To pry money from adventurers who were reluctant to complete payment on their shares, the London Company in 1612 got from the King a third and last charter, extending the bounds of its territory in America to include Bermuda and altering its organization to give effective control to the main body of adventurers, or investors, instead of to the Virginia council. Interest had shifted from ill-starred Virginia to the possibilities of Bermuda, and it was hoped that by tying the two together funds would be forthcoming not only to develop Bermuda but also to continue the support of the Virginia colony. Similarly, the decision to place control of both the company and the colony in the hands of the membership at large, retaining the council primarily to preserve the company's connection with the King, assured investors of a share in making decisions affecting their investment. Along with its efforts to make Virginia more attractive to investors through reforms instituted by the new charter, the Virginia council published in 1612 the legal code that had evolved under its direction in the past two years in Virginia, thereby offering assurances to prospective settlers that as Virginians they would live under a rule of laws, however stringent, and not of men.

In spite of all the company's efforts in 1612, interest in Virginia failed to revive. For the next four or five years the company had to forgo any thoughts of rapid expansion and content itself with giving the existing settlement what support it could out of proceeds from periodic Virginia lotteries. In the meantime, the colony, at peace with the Indians after the marriage of Pocahontas and John Rolfe in 1614, took on a certain air of stability and permanence. The settlers, few in number but well "seasoned" and ably led, pushed ahead with the job of clearing land, planting crops for their subsistence, and breeding farm animals to increase the small stock brought from England. The colonists lived in separate houses and planted their own gardens; but, unless they were officials or otherwise engaged in public work, as artisans or guards for instance, they were expected to labor under an overseer in the company's fields for a part of the morning and afternoon six days a week during the growing season. Some of these were employees of the company sent out at its expense to work the fields, but most were not. Until 1616, of course, the company retained possession of all land, had first call on all it produced, and supervised closely the entire operation of the colony. Everything that the company provided from England and all that the fields of the colony produced were supposed to go into a common store from which the colonists might draw rations, tools, and other supplies as needed. The company imposed this communal pattern of settlement only in part to fulfill the requirement of the joint stock of 1609 that profits earned and assets created before 1616 should be shared by all those who had invested their money or their labor. It also made it easier for the company to provide protection and support for those going out to the colony while making the most effective use possible of labor and supplies, both of which were scarce and obtainable only from England at great expense.

Even after 1616 when people had fulfilled their obligations to the joint stock and were embarking on private planting ventures, Virginia planters did not abandon the cooperative approach to land settlement. Until the company's demise, the usual practice was for groups of adventurers to pool funds, land, and labor when forming plantations. These early settlers, it should be noted, lacked certain advantages enjoyed by those who within a few years, and for many years thereafter, would be moving singly out onto the frontier. Their line of supply did not run back to a settlement only a few miles down the river but thousands of miles across the Atlantic. Nor did they have close behind them an established community to help roll back the Indians as new settlers advanced into the interior. And, while these early settlers brought with them the essential tools for clearing land and cultivating it (notably the iron ax and hoe) as well as some knowledge of farming techniques acquired on farms in Hampshire, Devon, or elsewhere, it was not for them just a matter of cutting down or girdling trees and cultivating the soil between the remaining stumps, as back-breaking a job as this was; they also had to learn through trial and error what to plant and when and how to plant it here in this strange climate of unexpected, and unpredictable, extremes of heat and cold, deluge and drought. It was a time for cooperation, and by working together the people of Jamestown prepared the base for the self-reliant, independent frontiersman to come.

By 1617 it was beginning to dawn on the Virginia adventurers in England that the colonists had at last learned what to plant and how. Tobacco was being raised in increasing quantities and shipped to England. It showed great promise of becoming a profitable staple for the Virginia economy, precisely what Virginia had long lacked and sorely needed. The year before, when the company had sought to make the first division of land under the terms of the expired joint stock by offering 50 acres near Jamestown to settlers entitled to a share and 100 acres per share to English investors provided they would now match their original investment by a like amount, few adventurers had taken up the offer. But in 1617 tobacco created a sudden interest in landholding in Virginia. Thereafter for the next six years the enthusiasm with which English adventurers claimed land and started plantations was the single most important factor in transforming Virginia from a static colony of less than 400 settlers to one of 4,500 settlers at the peak in 1622. Under the leadership of Sir Thomas Smith and Sir Edwin Sandys the company was quick to react to this new development. It increased its activities and altered its policies to encourage this interest in private planting, to accommodate the administration of the colony to its likely consequences, and to capitalize upon it so as to widen the scope of the company's own activities in Virginia. By 1618 the time seemed finally at hand for realizing the colony envisaged by the Hakluyts a generation before and by the leaders of the London Company certainly since 1611.

It was of first importance that the London Company should adopt a new land policy to encourage and sustain the awakening interest in private planting. To this end, in 1618 it offered every adventurer and old planter, as well as any servant of the company who had served in Virginia for seven years, 100 acres of land for each share held in the joint stock and another 100 acres as soon as the first hundred had been "sufficiently peopled," all rent free. Those immigrating after 1616 and at their own expense would on arrival receive 100 acres for themselves and an additional 100 for each person they then or subsequently brought out—the famous headright provision. Taken together, these provisions meant that a group of London adventurers considering investment in a plantation in Virginia began with 100 acres for each £12 10s. they invested in the joint stock; as soon as they should get workers on this acreage it would immediately be doubled and still another 100 acres would be added for every worker they sent out. Once land in America became valued, as it finally did in Virginia after a decade and at great cost in lives and money, it could be used to provide the incentive, the means, and the rewards for colonizing. And it was so used by Americans for two and one half centuries, in much the same way the London Company did, until the continent was filled and the United States stretched "from sea to shining sea." America was greatly blessed with land, but the getting it into the hands of many users was the genius of its development.

The company in 1618-1619 followed up the announcement of its new land policy with a number of other innovations to encourage the rapid settlement and development of Virginia. It did away with the harsh legal code of 1612 and, after reconfirming the guarantees of its charters that the colonists should retain all the rights of Englishmen, held out the promise of justice based on English common law and of its administration by colonial courts. It also gave to adventurers considerable authority in their "particular" or joint plantations, making them subject only to the laws of England, the regulations of the company, and the colony's government. To assure them that the policies of the company or the colony would not in the future take a turn destructive to their interests, planters were invited to sit in an assembly with the colonial governor and council to hear the petitions of the inhabitants, to make recommendations to the company in London, enact regulations for the government of the colony subject to the company's approval, and to review all company regulations affecting Virginia. So as not to load the adventurers and planters with burdensome taxes, the company proposed to operate public plantations manned by its employees, and out of the profits pay the salaries of public officials. No industry-starved town in the twentieth century could offer a wider range of inducements to a manufacturer seeking a site for a new plant, but its chamber of commerce would understand what the London Company was up to here in 1618.

The calling of a general assembly, like legal reform, was a move by the company in part to promote investment and settlement and in part "to reduce the people and affaires of *Virginia* into a regular course." It was the company's way of adapting colonial administration to the implications of private ownership of land and the accompanying growth of the colony. As Englishmen, they knew from experience that the best way to get the cooperation of people of property in maintaining good order and the security of society was to have their representatives meet regularly to devise ways and means to these ends. This was how the King got the cooperation of the adventurers as his subjects, and how the leading adventurers got the support of the members of the London Company for their policies.

The logic of using a representative assembly in governing Virginia was reinforced by requirements arising from the colony's increasing size, diversity, and extent. To implement its policies of fostering growth and prosperity by decentralizing authority and dispersing people through its disposition of land, the company proposed to establish four boroughs or townships to be points of concentration for settlement and units of local government coordinate with the "particular" plantations of adventurers, which would lie outside the boroughs. But growth had to be accommodated as well as fostered. If this new policy were not to defeat itself by fragmenting the expanding colony, the company had to act to preserve a semblance of colonial unity. An assembly of colonists representative of the parts but acting for and upon the whole was a device admirably suited to help maintain essential central authority without destroying local or private rights. And so it was that the twenty-two burgesses met in general assembly with Governor Francis Yeardley and six councilors in the church at Jamestown on July 30, 1619. This was not the last time in American politics that efforts to combat particularist tendencies threatening the general welfare would bear good fruit.

The London Company as such played an important role in all this under the imaginative leadership of Sir Edwin Sandys, who replaced Smith as treasurer early in 1619. Neither the knowledge that the company's new land policy wiped out its obligations to old settlers and investors and freed it of any obligation to pay for future settlements nor the fair prospects that its members would soon be drawing income from their private plantations lessened Sandys' determination to make the company both the promoter and the arbiter of the colony's future growth. There were the company's debt of upward of £9,000 and the adventurers' hardly satisfied hunger for profits to be considered. But more than these, here was the first real opportunity to make the colony what it should be, a prosperous and productive enterprise in America contributing directly to the prosperity and productivity of England.

In the spring of 1619 Sandys and his associates launched their program to use the company's lands in Virginia for the leavening that while stimulating its growth would convert Virginia into a model colony. Within less than two years, Sandys sent out well over 1000 men in the company's employ. Many of these had highly specialized skills. Recruited in Germany, Italy, and France as well as in England, they were to go to Virginia and develop new staples for the colony's economy by extracting from its soil and forests such things as iron, naval stores, timber, salt, drugs, and dyes. Other employees, including a few African Negroes brought to the colony by a Dutch sea captain in 1619, were put to work in the company's fields to experiment with the cultivation of indigo, cotton, silkworms, grapes, and similar marketable crops. Sandys hoped that by developing new staples like silk and wine the company could show the way for private planters to free themselves of their dangerous dependence upon tobacco, the future market for which was at the time highly uncertain. He hoped too that the success of the company's plantations and other ventures would permit the company to pay the salaries of colonial officials as it had promised and give financial support to religion and education in the colony, as well as make it possible for the company to pay its debts and perhaps dividends to the adventurers.

The immediate effect of Sandys' ambitious program was to stimulate private investments in Virginia. Scores of individuals and associated groups took out company patents to found plantations, and after the cancellation in 1621 of the Virginia lottery that had provided Sandys with the funds for his enterprises, most newcomers went as indentured servants to private plantations or, less often, as independent planters. One group receiving such a patent for trade and settlement in Virginia was composed of English separatists, living in Holland, who in 1620 landed and settled at Plymouth, by chance outside the bounds of Virginia. This little colony of people coming to America via Holland in order to separate themselves from the English church survived and prospered moderately until Plymouth was absorbed by Massachusetts in 1691. Its first governor, William Bradford, left the eloquent record of its early trials and triumphs, and through his *History* a new nation long after discovered its Pilgrim fathers.

During the two years after the Pilgrims landed at Plymouth all seemed to be going according to plan to the south in Virginia. Then, in 1622, the Indians drew themselves together and, as they were to do intermittently until the last tribe was subjugated in the nineteenth century, struck back at the invading Europeans, killing hundreds of settlers in outlying plantations. An outbreak of the plague in the next year killed hundreds more. When it was all over, only about 1200 settlers remained in Virginia. By 1623 the London Company was bankrupt and in disrepute. The King withdrew its charter in May 1624, and once again the fate of Virginia was in doubt.

The collapse of the company raised the dual question that had been faced before in one form or another in 1606, 1609, 1612, and

1618: How was Virginia to be supported and how governed? It had recently been getting support from the company's investments in the public estate, which was now to disappear in limbo, and from the adventurers' investments in their particular plantations, which most abandoned in despair after 1623. The British government quickly made it clear that it had no intention of taking up the slack. This left it to the people in Virginia; they would have to take on the job of supporting the colony as well as themselves. Because they did this, and because the English government failed to decide just what should be done about the governing of Virginia, they also had more say in shaping Virginia's new government than anyone in England had intended. The tough and seasoned planters who had survived the worst and learnt to wrest a competence from the soil now inherited Virginia and within a decade made it their own.

The indecision about how Virginia should be governed made it almost inevitable that the colony should continue to follow certain political forms and other procedures which had proved their utility under the company. The governor and council, now appointed, commissioned, and instructed by the King instead of by the company, continued to function as both administrative and judicial officers. This was the English government's interim answer to the immediate problem of preserving political authority in Virginia. But the governor and council, with the burgesses, also had since 1619 shared with the company the legislative function. The Virginia governor continued to have the assembly meet after 1624, at first occasionally and then annually, not so much because it had met under the company but because the English government's refusal to assume the supportive role of the company put a premium on public support for governmental policies in Virginia. The governor and council clearly found it useful to have the burgesses—Virginia planters elected to office by other planters—join with them in the conduct of public business: to raise money for government, to carry on the continuing war with the Indians, and to cope with the complex problems of tobacco as the staple of Virginia's economy. The English government at first only tolerated the assembly, not even officially acknowledging its existence until 1629, but in the 1630s the assembly established itself as an integral, even indispensable, part of colonial government. The King's instruction to the royal governor in 1639 to call the assembly each year was nothing more than the English government's recognition of this.

But the general question of support for Virginia involved something other than the crucial matter of fixing governmental forms to allow the colony to maintain order and meet its public charges. Behind this lay the original question of how to underwrite the development of an overseas colony—how to find the means to people it and make it productive. As soon as land in Virginia became a viable asset in 1618, the London Company had devised a system to use it to promote colonial development by offering land to anyone who could put it to good use. The King's governor in Virginia retained the company's head-right system of land distribution, parceling out additional acreage to old planters as they increased their families of children and servants, and conveying land to new planters when they applied for it. Virginia's land policy worked so well that by 1634, when the English government finally indicated its approval, the colony's population had more than quadrupled.

In fact, by 1634 Virginia had reached a size and complexity that demanded an elaboration of the rudimentary local government initiated earlier by the company with its "particular" plantations and monthly courts. The assembly, demonstrating its new-found competence and its will to govern, divided the colony into eight counties, established in each of these a monthly court manned by local magistrates holding commissions from the governor and council, and provided for a county sheriff, a clerk, constables, and a coroner to act as the court's officers. The long-vital militia was now organized by counties; and the parish vestry had even before 1634 been the subject of much legislation dealing with the crux of the problem—the minister's salary. All of this represented a deliberate effort to follow English forms in local government, but the planters of the assembly, wise in the ways of Virginia, defined these familiar county offices in terms not only of practices recollected from England but also of practices being followed in America. And the divergence from English models grew wider as the years passed. The county courts, whose magistrates individually and collectively performed both judicial and administrative functions, in time became the locus of power in colonial Virginia, the political base on which the power of the house of burgesses rested in its heyday in the eighteenth century.

In this way, the government under which Virginia functioned until the Revolution took form within ten years of the dissolution of the London Company that had done much to predetermine the form it should take. Hereafter there was to be a governor appointed by the king, a council appointed by him on the governor's recommendation, and a representative body elected by property-owning inhabitants: the three together making laws for the colony and two of them, the governor and council, acting as chief administrators of the laws and instructions of the Virginia assembly, British Parliament, and the king. There would also be a court system to enforce applicable laws and to assure conformity to English common law; local officials to manage the political, military, and religious affairs of the counties; and a land system designed to promote the expansion and prosperity of the colony. These were the basic elements of royal government in Virginia. The future was to bring shifts and adjustments, elaboration, innovation, and complication; but Thomas Jefferson would have found here much that was familiar, as would his contemporaries in other royal colonies. Although none of the thirteen colonies began as a royal one—that is, the British government as such did not plant any of them—by the time of the Revolution eight had a form of royal government like Virginia's, although differing in important details.

One of these pre-Revolutionary royal colonies, Massachusetts-Bay, was begun in 1630 as Virginia was working out its arrangements for living directly under the crown. For those seeking some understanding of America's origins, the story of the founding of Massachusetts is at least as important as the Virginia story.

Chapter IV

The Beginnings: Massachusetts

The push of the English into Virginia was part of a broad movement, essentially mercantile in motivation, which before 1630 also bore English colonists into Ireland, Newfoundland, Bermuda, Barbados, and New England. Shortly before the Pilgrims landed at Plymouth in 1620, Sir Ferdinando Gorges got from King James a charter transferring control of New England from the moribund Virginia Company of London and of Plymouth (1606) to a Council for New England composed of Gorges and a number of other landed aristocrats. Their object in securing the charter was not so much to promote trade and settlement in America as it was to establish great landed estates for themselves in New England, but the council did issue a number of patents for settlement during the 1620s. Among the patentees was a group of men from the port of Dorchester who in 1624 formed a joint-stock company to develop a fishing colony on the New England coast. Englishmen for many years had been fishing for cod in the waters off Newfoundland and northern New England, and the Dorchester men were keenly aware of the advantages it would give their city's fishing fleet to have a permanent settlement on the mainland. They hoped it might be used to provide supplies and additional fishermen for the fleet when it arrived from Dorchester each year.

The Dorchester Company supported a settlement of men at Cape Ann until 1626, when it became clear that the venture had failed, and the company broke up. After the Dorchester adventurers abandoned the project, the leading spirit in the venture from the beginning, the Reverend John White, turned to Puritans of standing and substance in London and the west country to secure support for the handful of Dorchester men who had hung on in New England. In 1628, these London merchants and country gentlemen enlisted by White formed a new joint-stock association to succeed the defunct Dorchester Company and, as the New England Company, got from Gorges' Council for New England a patent for settling the land lying between the Merrimack and the Charles. During the summer, the new company sent John Endecott with settlers and supplies to Salem, where the Dorchester remnant had moved from Cape Ann.

Although one of White's initial purposes in promoting the Dorchester venture had been to provide a minister for the fishermen who were in New England waters for most of each year, the coming together of London and west-country Puritans in the New England Company marked the introduction of a more distinctly religious element into the project for developing a fishing colony at Salem. Whether or not the adventurers in forming the company in 1628 actually had in mind the possibility of making Salem a haven for Puritans, the facts are that Puritans had become increasingly apprehensive about the drift of things in England since the death of James I in 1625, that the New England Company was an association of Puritans brought together for the purpose of promoting colonization in America, and that within twelve months of its inception the company had been converted into an instrument for establishing a new Puritan commonwealth in Massachusetts.

In the late 1620s Puritans in England watched with mounting alarm as doors through which they had hoped to pass since the days of Elizabeth were slammed shut one by one. For the first time they began to despair of ever rescuing the English church from the slough of error and corruption in which the Elizabethan Settlement of the previous century had left it. To all appearances, Charles I was set on a course that threatened to destroy the whole Puritan movement. By the late 1620s, however, Puritanism had been defining its purposes and gathering its strength for a half century and more. The Puritans were to be a more formidable opponent than the King knew.

The first "puritans" were those Elizabethans who became convinced that their queen had not gone nearly far enough in her reformation of the English church and were determined that its polity and dogma should soon be brought into line with God's dictates clearly laid down in Holy Scripture. As sinfully imperfect as it was to many, the Elizabethan church was nonetheless sufficiently Calvinist to accommodate, if not always easily, the vast majority of Puritans; and Anglican clergymen of the Puritan persuasion preached Puritan doctrine with relative freedom during the reigns of Elizabeth and her successor, James I. Elizabeth was most prone to crack down on Puritan divines at those times when she wished to remind her subjects that she would brook no tampering with the hierarchical form of church government to which the Puritans bitterly objected and through which she maintained her control. And James, although a Calvinist of sorts, followed her lead in this.

It was the freedom to preach the true faith that so long sustained the Puritans' high hopes that they would ultimately prevail. The sermons of the great preachers coming out of the university at Cambridge before and after the turn of the century fed the zeal for religious reform that was gripping a large segment of the English people; and the preachers converted many to Puritanism among the rich, well born, and powerful as well as among people of less exalted station. A measure of their effectiveness was the size of the Puritan contingent in Parliament where Puritans formed a strong minority and at times a majority in the last years of Elizabeth's reign and throughout James's. As Parliament during these years was growing in authority, the Puritans confidently expected that in a day not far off Parliament would purify the church and national life, saving England from the destruction God's wrath threatened. Charles I was not slow in putting an end to these high hopes and sanguine expectations after he came to the throne in 1625.

That the new king was married to a Roman Catholic princess was disquieting enough to Puritans, but what set the danger flags flying in the Puritan camp were Charles's intentions, soon made apparent, to curb the authority of Parliament and to favor the wing of the Anglican church most inimical to Puritan teachings. Charles's conflict with Parliament over taxes, should it lead to his dispensing with Parliament altogether, would end any chance for reform through legislation. As bad or worse were the implications of Charles's support of what the Puritans called the Arminian heresy in the Anglican church. This was the belief that man by his own efforts could attain faith and through faith, salvation—a bald rejection of a basic tenet of Calvinism. For the Anglican church to embrace this doctrine, as it seemed to be doing under William Laud, whom Charles made Bishop of London in 1628 and Archbishop of Canterbury in 1633, was to reverse the state's policy initiated by Elizabeth of defining church doctrine in a way to make it altogether possible for devout Puritans to remain in the church as nominal Anglicans.

The outlook had become dark indeed by early 1629 when the adventurers of the New England Company quietly secured a royal charter incorporating their company as the Massachusetts-Bay Company. The charter confirmed its right to the land in Massachusetts while freeing it of its former dependence upon the Council for New England. A month later, in April, the new company designated Endecott as its governor at Salem and sent out several hundred new settlers, mostly Puritans.

Although the Massachusetts-Bay Company was in late spring 1629 still a conventional trading corporation, its venture in New England rapidly took on, during the next few months, more and more the character of a refuge for Puritans. And for good reason. Times were bad both at home and abroad. The economic distress of England itself clearly signaled God's growing displeasure with this errant nation. The Thirty Years' War on the continent was going against the Protestant forces. And King and Parliament were on a collision course. Before the end of the year, Charles had again dissolved Parliament, this time letting it be understood that he proposed henceforth to rule without consulting the Lords and Commons. The great hope of Puritan reform had gone into sudden eclipse. The doctrinal position that the Anglican church was beginning to enforce under Laud was putting severe strain on the consciences of conforming Puritans, which most Puritans were, forcing them to ponder whether the hour was approaching when they would have to abandon their central purpose of redeeming the English church and take the dread step of separating themselves from it in order to save their own souls. As the King's favorite, Bishop Laud had also already begun to curtail the clergy's freedom to preach Puritan doctrine. If Puritans were to be denied the opportunity to enforce God's word through legislation and the freedom to reveal it through preaching, what was to become of Puritans and Puritanism, of their England and England's church caught up as they were in error and sin? These were questions that weighed heavily on the minds and hearts of many Puritans in the summer of 1629.

Among these troubled Puritans were twelve East Anglians, all men of standing and most of them members of the Massachusetts-Bay Company. In late August, at Cambridge, they agreed to go out with their families to Massachusetts, provided that "the whole government with the Patent [charter]" of the company be transferred to them before their departure. The royal charter of 1629, patterned after the London Company's charter of 1612, bestowed upon the membership of the Massachusetts-Bay Company the authority to manage its affairs and directed what form the company's government should take. The charter provided for a governor, a deputy governor, and 18 assistants, who were to meet four times a year in general court with the members of the company—the freemen—to elect officers, admit new members, and make laws for the company and its colony. After considerable debate, the company took the momentous step of handing over the charter to John Winthrop and his fellow East Anglians. Winthrop took over as governor in the early fall of 1629 to arrange for the removal of the company from London to Massachusetts, which was accomplished in 1630.

A number of important things had happened here, things that were to make the way of colonizing Massachusetts very different from the earlier way in Virginia. The transfer of the charter to Winthrop and his colleagues going out to Massachusetts meant that planters in Massachusetts, not adventurers in London, would govern both company and colony. The inherent logic of this was that the two, company and colony, would in short order become one and the same: colonial government would be, in form and substance, the government authorized for the company by the charter. This is what happened, not all at once but within less than a decade as the generality of inhabitants in Massachusetts first attained the status of freemen in the colony and then, as freemen, claimed and step by step made good their right under the charter to elect the governor, deputy governor, and assistants and to have their deputies sit with these officials in general court to make all laws for the colony. In Virginia, it was twelve years—in 1619 at the first meeting of the general assembly—before colonial government approximated even the form of the company's government in London, and at least that much longer before it had the approximate authority in the colony that the London Company had exercised before its dissolution. Even then Virginia did not enjoy the corporate existence that gave Massachusetts such a wide area of freedom from royal control for half a century until its charter was revoked in 1684.

Nothing demonstrates better that Virginia and Massachusetts were founded under very different auspices and for quite different purposes than the fact that Jamestown was for long closely supervised from London while in Massachusetts authority immediately passed to the colony. Men of affairs engaged in a mercantile venture like that in Virginia must retain control if they are to realize a profit; men of God to advance His kingdom in Massachusetts had to put into the hands of His magistrate there the authority to enforce His will. One rather strange by-product of the immediate transfer of political control to Massachusetts, and of its long delay in coming to Virginia, was that the first generation of political leaders in Massachusetts owed their position of leadership largely to their former standing in English society whereas in Virginia they owed it to their proven ability to scratch out for themselves a place in the wilderness. Democratic-to-be Massachusetts was founded and nurtured by Englishmen who were gentlemen; aristocratic-to-be Virginia was rescued after the London Company's demise and got going again by Americans, and hard-bitten frontiersmen at that.

Nevertheless, the governments of the two colonies, both derived from trading corporations, were basically the same in structure. Between them they set the pattern for government in the English colonies that were to follow, and they stand as the direct ancestors of the present corporate form of both federal and state government in the United States. The most important political principle that the trading corporation introduced into colonial government in Virginia and in Massachusetts was the principle of representation. And it was representation based directly on what may be called a person's stake, interest, or investment in the colonizing venture—land holding, and by inference its cultivation, in Virginia, and membership in the Puritan church in Massachusetts. No matter how imperfect the two modes of representation may seem to a later generation, both constituted a broadening and rationalizing of the representative principle as compared to the prevailing mode in Parliament.

The fixing of church membership instead of landholding as the passport to full participation in colonial government suggests a second important consequence of the decision to transfer the charter and company from London to Massachusetts. In one stroke Winthrop and his friends had completed the transformation of the Massachusetts project from a traditional colonizing venture with trade as its object into a venture of a different sort in which the founding of a religious community had become the objective. The broad purpose of planting Virginia had been to satisfy national goals, to promote the good of the nation; but the planting of Massachusetts if successful would glorify God and advance His Kingdom on earth by setting a city upon a hill for a beacon to Christendom. While it is true that individuals came to Massachusetts, just as they had come to Virginia, for varied and mixed reasons, there cannot be the least doubt that the wish to share in creating a godly community was the transcendent motive for the great migration of Puritans to Massachusetts in the 1630s. What the Puritans sought they found only imperfectly, but in the seeking they set the initial and unique form of their society and its institutions.

Specifically, the Puritans came to Massachusetts to make of themselves a viable community held together by Christian love and dedicated to the enforcement of God's will. Their building blocks they knew to be poor stuff. Born sinful and corrupt like all men, the Puritans held no hope that by their efforts alone they could achieve any good or avoid the eternal damnation they so richly deserved. But as Christians they took heart from the knowledge that set against the ineradicably sinful nature of man was the perfection of God's wisdom, power, and holiness. Available to them in the Bible were God's instructions for man. With their God-given reason they could learn from it precisely what it was that God intended them to do in all things. And God in His infinite mercy had revealed that He had singled out a chosen few of His fallen creatures for salvation. From God's chosen in Massachusetts, from His saints, from the elect, would be drawn those of higher station and wider experience to guide and govern the colony, to serve as its spiritual and political leaders. Those who were ministers would insure that the people understood God's commands aright; those who like Winthrop were magistrates would enforce His commands, seeking out and punishing any and all infractions of God's laws. So encouraged and so supported, every man and woman of this Puritan commonwealth who thirsted for God's grace, for eternal salvation, would strive with unremitting zeal to bring under God's discipline his own sinful nature and, in Christian love, that of his neighbor. God's will would be done, and He would make Massachusetts to prosper.

The Puritan experiment in Massachusetts derives its importance not so much from any peculiarities of religious dogma which set Massachusetts apart from Anglicanism on the one side and Separatism on the other, for, differing from them at certain points though it did, Puritanism shared with both most of its fundamental assumptions about the nature of God and his relationship to man. Nor was it so much the intensity with which the Puritans of Massachusetts held their beliefs. Laud was as dedicated an Anglican as Winthrop was a Puritan, and the separatist sects gave no odds to Massachusetts Puritans in their piety and their religious zeal. What in fact gives the Puritan experiment in Massachusetts its peculiar significance is the fixity of purpose with which its early leaders struggled to impose upon a whole society an incredibly comprehensive and excruciatingly demanding pattern of thought and conduct. This was no winnowing of saints from the world to preserve their sanctity; even less was Massachusetts a haven for saints to pursue privately and independently their personal salvation. God's biblical instructions were directed to all men, not just to those He had elected to save, and all men were bound to obey in fear of God's just wrath. In order to enforce God's will, as they must, the Puritans had to remain in the world, not separate from it; they had to take the world as they found it, as God made it, sinful and corrupt, and wage ceaseless battle against sin and corruption. The crank which tightened the coil of American Puritanism, storing the energy that was to infuse and permeate American life and character, was the impossible but inescapable necessity of imposing God's perfect law on an imperfect world. The key to the historical importance of the Puritans of Massachusetts is not that they sought God but that, in seeking Him, they became their brother's keeper.

The Puritans' vision of a commonwealth under God's dominion, in retrospect still both exalting and terrifying, radical almost beyond belief, depended for its realization upon certain practical assumptions that proved to be of doubtful validity. Winthrop and his associates assumed—had to assume—that God's instructions were clear and unambiguous, that men of learning and true faith would know, and would agree upon, what He intended in every eventuality. The fact is, of course, that the words of the Bible are often ambiguous, even contradictory; and Massachusetts Puritans equally learned and devout did on many occasions disagree about God's revealed intentions. More than once their disagreements threatened to split the colony, which would have endangered its existence and made a mockery of what it was meant to represent. Orthodoxy was maintained only at the cost of introducing a coercive note where none was intended and of driving from Massachusetts some of its most gifted people. The early Puritan leaders also assumed that as they died out their progeny, nurtured in this godly commonwealth and filled with zeal for the holy experiment, would replace them. But this was not to be. The founding fathers spent their declining years trying to cope with the growing worldliness of their offspring and lamenting the passage of the old days of Winthrop and John Cotton.

Shortly after Governor Winthrop and the other officers of the company landed at Salem in June 1630 with about 700 people, circumstances forced them to make a number of decisions of a practical nature that had little specific reference to their larger purpose but were to affect it fundamentally. Several of these decisions also contrasted sharply with those made earlier for Virginia by the London Company, with the result that the Massachusetts pattern from the outset was very different from Virginia's.

After a brief stay in Salem, the newcomers under Winthrop's direction set up temporary quarters on the Charlestown peninsula between the Mystic and Charles rivers and on Massachusetts Bay. While Winthrop, Deputy Governor Thomas Dudley, and the ten or so assistants who came to Massachusetts debated the proper site for permanent settlement, many of their people, weakened by the long voyage, came down with the bloody flux and scurvy; and it was rumored that the French were planning to attack them. Feeling that under the circumstances they must immediately abandon their cramped and exposed position on the peninsula, the leaders of the colony decided to disperse. The colony then broke up into a number of small settlements around the bay and on the banks of its rivers.

The absence of any threat from powerful Indian tribes made this policy of dispersal feasible; the subsequent great inflow of English settlers who built up the various settlements, or towns, and bought the produce of the old settlers allowed it to succeed. As defense did not require that the early colonists stick together, and as the basic problem of supply (that is, of capitalization), was almost automatically solved for them by the steady Puritan migration, a concentration of settlement for a prolonged period, like that at Jamestown, was for Massachusetts not only unnecessary but inappropriate, not to say impossible.

The immediate and rapid dispersal of population in Massachusetts resulted in a pattern of settlement that was compact and orderly when compared with what evolved in Virginia after the experiment in communal living at Jamestown was finally abandoned. Most people coming to New England in the 1630s could and did settle in fairly close proximity to fellow colonists. The governor and assistants of Massachusetts-Bay ordered, as need required, the laying out of a succession of townships along the coast and into the interior. Only the land falling within the boundaries of one of these towns was made available for settlement. This policy of grouping the population in a series of contiguous settlements facilitated the raising and marketing of foodstuffs and held saint and sinner alike within easy reach of a Puritan meetinghouse. It also preserved in New England some remnants of the familiar English village, no real trace of which had survived in Virginia. By the time the Puritans arrived in Massachusetts the Virginians were living on isolated farms widely scattered along and back from scores of rivers and streams in the tidewater. The same necessity that had decreed the concentration of settlement at Jamestown plantation until about 1618 thereafter forced first the London Company and then the colony of Virginia to offer vacant land at random to any man who would take it up. Virginia developed its public land policy to meet the colony's chronic need for settlers; the leaders of the Bay Colony, on the other hand, were able to use the fact of the steady migration to Massachusetts in the 1630s to direct the province's land policy toward the achievement of desired social ends.

Each of the English colonies, and after 1776 the states and the federal government, used either Virginia's head-right system of granting land to individuals or the Massachusetts policy of blocking out townships for immediate occupation by settlers in number—or some variant or combination of the two—to convey public land to millions of individuals for their private use and ownership. As dissimilar as they were, the public land policies of Massachusetts and Virginia served the same basic purpose, and served it well, by planting European farmers on American soil. The growth and dispersal of population fostered by the availability of land also created for each colony, and later for the other colonies as well, certain like problems in political administration. In every instance colonial administrators found their task taking on new dimensions once people began to move away from the point of initial settlement. It was no simple matter to maintain control from the center while extending farther and farther the limits of settlement. One facet of American politics has always been the push and pull between a territorial whole and its component parts.

Certainly the rapid dispersal of settlement in Massachusetts-Bay Colony forced other decisions that in turn greatly complicated the task of the colony's leaders. Their prime duty was to establish under the charter the firm authority of the colonial government, and through it to impose the unity of purpose that alone would allow the Puritan commonwealth to prosper and fulfill its self-appointed mission. Once the inhabitants were scattered, this of course became more difficult to achieve. Worse yet, the new pattern of settlement left the Massachusetts government with no choice but to make some provision for government in the separate towns even at the risk of raising up rivals to its own authority.

The governor and assistants, acutely aware of what their decision to move the people out from the encampment at Charlestown implied, kept a tight rein on the dispersal as they sent the people off in groups to settle together at designated sites. Apparently the colony's leaders tried to see to it that an assistant went along with each group, for on August 30 the board of assistants made six of their number justices of the peace to act as chief judicial and administrative officers in the six plantations, or towns, where they were to live. The advantages of having the men who collectively formed the government of the colony serve in their individual capacities as instruments of local government were so immediately apparent that it became the practice to make every new assistant a justice, or magistrate as he was soon called. The local magistrate's status as an assistant lent to him the prestige and authority he needed to maintain good government in the town. Individual magistrate-assistants also became in effect agents of the general government in the localities, facilitating the enforcement of colonial policy and minimizing the tendency of local government to dilute the authority of general government and thereby loosen the crucial bonds of colonial unity.

The decision of Winthrop and the assistants to lay out towns for settlement rather than to open up land at random was closely connected to the central purpose of the Puritan migration—the establishment of a Bible commonwealth. If Massachusetts was to become such a commonwealth, the church clearly must be its key institution. Every inhabitant must live near a house of worship and under the watchful eye of minister and godly neighbors, not off alone in some remote clearing. Circumstances decreed that those coming to Massachusetts could and must immediately spread beyond the confines of Winthrop's peninsula, but it was the Puritan design that required they go not singly but together and form towns.

On the other hand, if the centrality of religion to the Massachusetts experiment helped predetermine the pattern of settlement, the pattern that settlement took in turn did much to fix the form of organization of the New England church. One thing about which the Massachusetts Puritans were agreed, as were all Puritans, was that the Anglican form of church government, with its hierarchy descending from king through archbishops, bishops, and priests, was without Biblical authority. Puritans differed, however, about what form the Bible did authorize, some favoring leaving each congregation independent, others wishing to combine the individual churches into presbyteries and the presbyteries into synods in order to assure greater doctrinal and procedural uniformity. Any doubts about which way Massachusetts would go in this were soon removed. It was in the summer of 1630, not long after people had gone out to form settlements around the bay, that Governor Winthrop and the assistants made known their choice of church government for Massachusetts: it was to be the congregational form rather than the presbyterian one.

Whether the leaders of the venture had decided this before setting sail from England or whether the examples of the functioning congregational church at Salem and the independent churches of Plymouth influenced their decision after they arrived, the plan and rate of settlement during its first decade rendered congregationalism the more suitable if not the only practicable form of church organization for the colony. What with the rapid growth and equally rapid dispersal of the population, the hard-pressed managers of colonization in its primitive stages had little choice but to leave it to each locality to establish and maintain its own church. A nucleus of saints in a new town could form a congregation, seek a minister of the true persuasion if there was not one among them, and then see to it that all inhabitants were properly instructed in God's word and properly punished for any transgression of His law. There was, to be sure, always the weight of the united opinion of the colony's ministers and the authority of its government to be brought to bear upon a wayward congregation or an erring minister. Even so, several times during the 1630s it was touch and go whether the combination of lay and clerical pressure would suffice to maintain Puritan orthodoxy. The response of some congregations to the unorthodox teachings of Roger Williams and of Anne Hutchinson served to expose the inherent contradiction between congregational independence and perfect orthodoxy, very nearly destroying the Massachusetts colony in the process.

In the end, however, congregationalism proved flexible enough, and vulnerable enough, to allow the political authorities to act at critical junctures to isolate and excise religious error, and to do it without causing the internal schism that might have resulted if error had been free to percolate through presbyteries erected overnight. Underlying all of this is the indisputable fact that the congregational approach eased the way for the church to become the essential unifying force in the building of communities in which Puritan and non-Puritan alike lived and sometimes prospered.

Whatever the precise connection between the decision to form towns and the decision to adopt congregationalism, once acted upon they together brought into being what became the distinctive feature of local government in the new commonwealth: the town meeting. The emergence of this institution provides the plainest clue to the nature of the society that was forming in Massachusetts in the 1630s. Unlike the magistracy, it had no real counterpart in England nor did it appear in Virginia or any of the other colonies except those spawned by Massachusetts in New England. In the first settlements on Massachusetts Bay, town and congregation were hardly distinguishable. A large proportion of the earliest settlers were church members and those who were not were required to attend all services in the meetinghouse. Congregational meetings provided the opportunity for the inhabitants to discuss the overlapping problems of church and community. As the church became more institutionalized and its membership more restricted, congregational meetings served less well as public forums, and separate meetings began to be called regularly to deal with general town matters. These, of course, were the famous town meetings.

The New England town meeting has a history of its own. In time, agencies and officials of the meeting came to perform certain public services and to conduct much of the public business. The meeting also at some times and at some places lost the initiative in setting public policy to the selectmen it chose to manage the town's affairs. But the meeting itself remained a vital element in town life. Even when it lost the initiative, it continued to serve a unique purpose. It offered to the generality of inhabitants the frequent opportunity to have their say, by word or, at election time, by vote, about the policies adopted and about the officials carrying them out. Though subject to manipulation and domination like any other such public body, the New England town meeting was the most remarkable if not the most influential institution to emerge in early America.

It should be noted, too, that the extent of the town's political authority within the colony at large was considerable. For instance, the town quickly became the agency for distributing land to settlers. The governor and assistants always issued the patent that set the geographical limits of a new town, but the towns gained the right to parcel out the land within their boundaries to individuals according to a fixed pattern and formula. The county court in Virginia, on the other hand, never exercised this important power: the granting of land in that colony remained the jealously guarded prerogative of the royal governor and his council.

The sum of all this is that the essential forms and procedures of local government, civil and religious, had emerged in Massachusetts and the basic relationship between the localities and the provincial government had been worked out by about the time counties and parishes appeared in Virginia in the mid-1630s. It was mainly because of the differing rates and patterns of settlement that local government, evidence both of growing social complexity and of greater social stability, evolved so much more quickly in Massachusetts than in Virginia. By bringing men and money into Massachusetts on a scale that dwarfed the earlier efforts of the London Company, migrating Puritans in five years carried Massachusetts to the proximate level of development that Virginia reached only after a quarter of a century of arduous labor. It is not enough to note that England's colonies in America were settled at different times and under differing circumstances; one must also take into account the unevenness of their growth in order to explain otherwise inexplicable similarities and differences.

Although life for the Puritans in the New World defined itself in terms of the day-to-day existence of individuals living in such places as Watertown, Roxbury, Dorchester, Hingham and, of course, Boston, Governor Winthrop and the provincial officers provided the context in which towns formed and then existed in some mutual harmony and safety. Their main concerns were with defense, the economy, the maintenance of order, and in all of these and above all else with securing conformity to God's plan for these His people as it unfolded in the Massachusetts-Bay Colony. By bringing the charter with them, Winthrop and the assistants assured themselves of a free hand in Massachusetts insofar as their coreligionists in England were concerned. Far more important, the removal of the charter from England to Massachusetts opened the way for Winthrop to convert the main body of Puritans in the colony into a functioning partner of their leaders in the great venture. It is difficult to see how Massachusetts could have gone as far as it did toward realizing its ideal if Winthrop had not been able to achieve this.

As the only members of the company in Massachusetts in 1630, the governor and assistants under the terms of the charter could have ruled the colony as a self-perpetuating oligarchy had they chosen to do so. Instead, at a meeting in the fall of 1630 they announced that the "freemen" in the colony should elect the assistants, who in turn would, as before, elect the governor and deputy governor. Freemen were by definition simply members of the company, but in Massachusetts the designation was made to mean all adult male members of the Puritan church. By extending freemanship to those who came out to join him in building a city upon a hill for Christendom, Winthrop immediately achieved what the London Company had intended to move toward in 1612 when it assigned stock in the company to settlers at Jamestown in order to give them a stake in the enterprise. By the act of choosing the assistants each year the freemen would, it was supposed, annually affirm their assent to the rule of their godly rulers and their pledge of obedience to them. The leaders of the Bay Colony had found in their custody of the charter a way to gain popular sanction for the authority the charter legally bestowed upon them.

But this was not the end of it. The charter in fact provided that the freemen, the members of the company, should meet in general court four times a year with the governor and assistants to make all laws for the company and colony. At one of these meetings the freemen were supposed to elect not only the assistants but the governor and deputy governor as well. Anticipating demands of the freemen, Winthrop in 1632 got the assistants to agree to let the freemen elect the governor and deputy governor. At the same time the freemen were invited to send once a year to the general court two deputies from each town to consult with the governor and assistants about taxes. Then, in 1634, the town deputies asked to see the charter. When Governor Winthrop reluctantly complied with this demand, the people of the colony learned for the first time the full extent of the powers the charter conferred on the freemen.

The reaction to the disclosure of the terms of the charter was swift and decisive. In the election court of 1634 the freemen showed their displeasure by refusing to reelect Winthrop as governor, choosing Thomas Dudley instead. Their deputies also got the governor and assistants to agree to allow them to participate henceforth in all deliberations of the general court. In the long run this proved to be a fundamental alteration of the colonial constitution, but in the years immediately succeeding, John Winthrop and his associates, who had supervised the Massachusetts experiment from the start, continued to direct the building of the new Zion. They did so, however, with an awareness even keener than before of the prime importance of maintaining popular support for their rule.

The severest challenge to Winthrop's vision of a union of saints, a community in which God's will would be rightly understood and scrupulously enforced, was to come, however, not from any popular discontent with the management of affairs of state by the governor and assistants but from doubts raised about their proper understanding of God's revealed purposes. In the mid-1630s, first Roger Williams and then Anne Hutchinson espoused doctrines that in effect denied that the magistrates were enforcing God's will in Massachusetts. The great danger in each case was that the words of false teachers might breed general disagreement about what God intended. For the founders of Massachusetts to tolerate within the commonwealth conflicting views about the nature of God's rule was in effect to concede that the colony had no special mission. The Williams and the Hutchinson crises tested not only the mettle of Winthrop and the other leaders of the colony but also the validity of the assumptions upon which the whole Massachusetts experiment rested.

It was Roger Williams' alarming success at Salem in luring the unwary into the snares of separatism with his beguiling sermons and transparent goodness that first aroused the government in Boston to action. Unable to win him over or to silence him, the rulers of the colony forced Williams into exile in 1636. Williams and his band were hardly off for Rhode Island when Boston was thrown into an uproar by the antinomian teachings of the remarkable Anne

Hutchinson. Once again the colony's magistrates confronted a fo-
menter of false doctrine and put her down, sending Mrs. Hutchinson and the unrepentant among her followers out of the colony in
1637. Winthrop's brand of religious orthodoxy had been upheld
and the unity of the Puritan community in Massachusetts maintained, but at a high cost.

As the number of inhabitants swelled to upwards of perhaps
10,000 toward the end of the colony's first decade, a growing
unease about the paternalistic character of the colony's government
manifested itself even among the most godly. There was general
satisfaction with the "New England Way" given definition over the
years by decisions made and practices followed under the benign
guidance of John Winthrop, but more and more people concluded
that the time had come to institutionalize, to depersonalize, what
wise leadership had wrought. In 1641, despite Winthrop's misgiv-
ings, the general court adopted a "Body of Liberties," providing
for the first time a code of laws for the colony. The code was in a
sense a detailed description of the New England Way as followed
in the past and to be held to in the future. No longer would the
freemen of Massachusetts have to rely solely on the wisdom and
self-restraint of its rulers for good government and the preservation
of their liberties. There were now laws set down to guide and
restrain the magistrates and to inform the people of their just rights.

The people were also to have a greater say in any new laws that
might be made in the future. Their deputies finally got out from
under the domination of the governor and assistants in the general
court in 1644 when they established their right to sit separately at
the meetings of the court. The deputies had come to the point of
doing what the Virginia burgesses had done in the 1620s by making themselves the third branch of the legislature, distinct from the
governor and from the assistants and sharing fully in the law-mak-
ing process. The magistrates henceforth found themselves not only
hedged in by a code of laws but also watched over and competed
with by the people's representatives. And not being royal officials
like their counterparts in Virginia, the governor and assistants were
unable to oppose the pretensions of the popular assembly by invok-
ing the authority of the king.

It was fortunate that the Massachusetts system of government and politics had taken firm shape by the early 1640s and that it rested upon a broad base of popular support, for after the King reconvened Parliament in 1640 events moved rapidly in England to bring about, among many other things, drastic changes in the Massachusetts situation. The ensuing struggle between the English Puritans and Charles I, culminating in civil war, abruptly checked the flow of people to Massachusetts and led some of the Puritans in the colony to return home. The main thrust of the Puritan movement had shifted from Massachusetts back to England.

The loss after 1640 of the sense of being the mecca for all Puritans undoubtedly blunted the thrust of the Massachusetts experiment and turned it in upon itself, leaving the saints apprehensive and confused. More immediately critical, however, was the loss of customers, the disappearance of ships bringing new immigrants with money to buy the produce of the old settlers. With the main outlet for their products gone and consequently without the money to pay for the English goods they required, the people of Massachusetts found themselves in dire economic straits. It became essential that they find outside markets for their surplus fish, grain, livestock, and other local products. They were not long in doing so. Soon ships were abuilding to carry produce to waiting customers on the islands of the West Indies and beyond. Massachusetts was discovering that its economic salvation lay in overseas trade. It was yet to learn the threat this posed to the purity and integrity of the little Bible commonwealth fashioned by its founding fathers.

Chapter V

The Old British Empire

The first stage of English colonization in North America came to an end in the early 1640s when the prolonged struggle between Charles I and the House of Commons reached the point of no return and England descended into civil war. As the forces of the Puritans and Parliament first fought and then triumphed over the forces of the King, the flow of settlers into Massachusetts dropped to a trickle, and English officials were unable to pay much attention to the colonies. After the monarchy was restored in 1660 the English government, prodded by those interested in the expansion of trade, moved to exploit the potentialities of English North America. Parliament enacted a series of trade regulations, or Navigation Acts, designed to increase England's self-sufficiency, and hence her wealth, by systematically excluding foreigners from trade within the empire and by channeling trade with the outside through England itself.

The first two of the Navigation Acts, those of 1660 and 1663, defined the role of colonies in the great commercial empire that the English sought in the seventeenth century and gained and lost in the eighteenth. The colonies were to ship specified staples of their farms and forests to England for consumption or for foreign sale and to buy the goods they required from English merchants. And all such trade would be conducted in British ships manned by British seamen. The basic assumption from which these acts of trade sprang—that colonies existed for the benefit of the mother country

—underlay Britain's colonial policy from the planting of Virginia until the American Revolution. And the rationale for proceeding on this assumption was always that whatever contributed to the power and wealth of the mother country would ultimately benefit her dependents overseas.

The persistent search by the English government for ways and means to give reality to this commercial or mercantile empire first conceived by the Hakluyts and their sixteenth-century contemporaries, launched by the London adventurers at Jamestown, and given statutory definition by the Navigation Acts, was perhaps the main determinant of American development in the last four decades of the seventeenth century. A generation of English officials after 1660 struggled to impose upon the colonists a pattern of trade that altered old and more profitable arrangements, particularly with the Dutch. They simultaneously sought to promote the growth of English America and to increase its productivity, for the value to the mother country of engrossing colonial produce and of monopolizing colonial markets depended upon what and how much her colonists produced and were able to buy.

To make any progress in enforcing far-reaching economic regulations in the face of stubborn resistance and at a distance of 3000 miles required the creation, both in England and America, of new political agencies, techniques, and concepts, and the reshaping of old ones. That is, the machinery for building and maintaining an extended commercial empire had to be constructed, set in motion, and repeatedly adjusted to meet the ever-changing realities of conditions in America. The great achievement of England's seventeenth-century empire builders was in defining and institutionalizing the complex relationships between the mother country and her colonies in a way that permitted for half a century and more an approximate realization of the aims of empire as set out by the Navigation Acts. By 1700, most of the procedures and agencies the British used to administer the empire at its zenith in the eighteenth century were fixed. And within this framework the thirteen colonies grew and prospered until ready to make good their bid for independence after 1776.

The elaboration of the machinery of imperial administration was clearly both a cause and a consequence of what was certainly the most striking development in English America in the latter part of the seventeenth century—its rapid extension along the Atlantic seaboard. The English planted new colonies up and down the coast and established effective control of the coastline from Maine to Spanish Florida. Great men in London intimately involved in directing England's renewed bid for empire, among them Sir Anthony Ashley Cooper, later the Earl of Shaftesbury, secured a charter from King Charles II in 1663 to establish a colony in the Carolinas; and by 1680 there were organized communities of settlers centering around Albemarle Sound to the north and Charles Town (Charleston) to the south. In 1664 the English wrested New Amsterdam from the Dutch; and James, Duke of York, Charles II's brother and himself King from 1685 to 1688, took the territory for his own and called it New York. A part of it, New Jersey, he gave to his friends John Lord Berkeley and Sir George Carteret, two of Ashley Cooper's associates in the Carolina enterprise. A few years later William Penn got from King Charles a charter to settle the region between Jersey and Maryland, and in 1682 launched his extraordinarily successful colony in Pennsylvania.

In the meantime, the older colonies were expanding along the coast and into the interior. From the first years of its settlement, immigrants to Massachusetts had ventured out, or been driven out, of the Puritan commonwealth of Massachusetts-Bay to other parts of New England. Puritan communities existed as far away as Long Island well before 1660. The Connecticut settlements secured royal recognition of their independent existence in 1662, as did those in Rhode Island in 1663. Charters from the King empowered the inhabitants in each of these two colonies to erect and maintain governments of their own choosing. And to the south, the two Chesapeake colonies of Maryland and Virginia were already beginning to taste the joys and woes of the plantation societies they were to become.

Obviously much of this colonizing activity by the English after 1660 derived from the same expansive mercantile and imperial impulse that was impelling the English to give suitable form to the emerging empire. The acquisition of New York and the colonizing of Carolina are cases in point. But by the same token it was precisely this dramatic extension of English settlements that made urgent the need for closer supervision and tighter control of the colonies from London. The English were facing up to, and not for the last time, the central problem in imperial administration: how to maintain the indispensable unity of an empire in the face of the proliferation and growth of its colonies. The more numerous, the more populous, and the more productive England's colonies became after 1660, the nearer Britain approached fulfillment of her mercantile ambitions; but every step toward fulfillment increased both the difficulty and urgency of the central government's asserting its authority throughout the empire. All would be lost if the imperial government were not competent to keep the peace within the parts and to secure the whole from outside enemies. Bit by bit, and often haphazardly, the English devised their solution to this problem of imperial order. It was not until after the French and Indian War in the 1750s that these arrangements worked out in the late seventeenth century no longer seemed to answer the purpose. It was then that Britain embarked upon a disastrous reorganization of her American empire, which ended with the Americans themselves assuming the task of providing security and order for their country.

The authority of the English government was extended to seventeenth-century America through the prerogatives, or magisterial powers, of the king. Obedience by the colonists to the dictates of government, whether that government was English or colonial, was demanded and given in the name of the king. Working within the framework of Parliament's acts of trade, the king and his officers with increasing purpose and efficiency after 1660 set colonial policy, created colonial offices, appointed colonial officials, formulated procedures, issued directives, enforced those acts of Parliament applicable to the colonies, and generally supervised the operation of the empire. Instead of many new administrative agencies appearing to handle colonial affairs, the tendency was for existing ones to expand their traditional functions to include America. Charles II's Privy Council, for example, was arbiter of the colonies until his death in 1685, and thereafter it continued to act with or for the king to give his sanction to royal directives, review colonial legislation, and serve as the court of last resort for the colonists. The secretary of state for the southern department added the American colonies to southern Europe as the area of his special responsibility.

The ships of the Admiralty and the customs service of the Treasury began to play in America their familiar roles in the enforcement of trade regulations. In 1696 William III created the Board of Trade as a permanent board of experts to coordinate royal supervision of the colonies. The board kept itself informed of developments in America, made recommendations for action to the appropriate executive agencies in London, and transmitted advice and instructions to royal officials in America.

The royal establishment that functioned within the several colonies varied widely, both in nature and extent. Only in royal colonies like Virginia did the king appoint a governor and council to govern in cooperation with a locally elected assembly. But all of the colonies, even chartered and proprietary ones, in time had in residence officials appointed by the king to aid in the enforcement of the trade regulations. These included such officers as collectors of the customs, surveyors of the customs, and naval officers. After 1697 when an act of Parliament provided for establishing vice-admiralty courts in America, royal officials in every colony were legally empowered to prosecute violators of the acts of trade in the courts of the king. In the proprietary colonies the king otherwise had to depend largely upon the proprietors to defend the interests and assert the authority of the mother country. And in granting the charters to Connecticut and Rhode Island, Charles chose, for reasons that remain inexplicable and in any case ill-founded, to rely largely upon the inhabitants of these colonies to uphold British colonial policy.

In the 1670s and 1680s when the Privy Council was working to give form and direction to England's burgeoning American empire, it took steps that indicate there was a movement afoot to introduce in the chartered and proprietary colonies the pattern of royal government that had evolved in Virginia after the collapse of the London Company in the 1620s. Greater uniformity in colonial government and more direct control of colonial affairs by the crown was the object. The shift to royal government was achieved in Massachusetts in the 1680s and 1690s after the revocation of its charter under which it had functioned as a more or less independent commonwealth since its founding over half a century before. The movement toward uniformity and centralization reached its climax when James II became King in 1685 and created the Dominion of

New England. The Dominion, which placed the colonies of New England under a single royal governor and abolished their elected assemblies, was to be the first step in erasing old colonial boundaries and organizing English America into new regional administrative units governed by royal officials.

The Revolution of 1688 driving James from the throne brought the brief Stuart experiment in colonial consolidation and centralization to an abrupt end. But the new king, William of Orange, was as interested as his predecessor in perfecting colonial administration and in confirming royal authority in America. It was during his reign (1689-1702) that most of the finishing touches were put on the imperial structure that held up rather well under the strain of rapid colonial growth until Parliament attempted to overhaul it in the 1760s. Although William confirmed the old colonial charters, and neither he nor his successors made any concerted effort to convert the proprietary or chartered colonies into royal ones, all of the mainland American colonies except Pennsylvania, Maryland, Rhode Island, and Connecticut had royal governments when the French and Indian War broke out in 1754.

It is both odd and important that the fundamental shift in power within the English government from king to Parliament, begun by the expulsion of James II and confirmed when the Hanoverian George I was called to the throne in 1713, did not in fact carry over into colonial administration. British authority in America continued to be exerted through the king, and it was against the royal prerogative that the colonial politicians of the eighteenth century fought whenever they undertook to extend the powers of the elected assemblies in the colonies or to defend individual rights claimed by the colonists. Parliament found no cause to challenge or diminish royal authority in the colonies, for William and the chief ministers of succeeding monarchs were as avid as any member of the House of Commons to promote the mercantile aims of the empire. When Parliament did at last, after 1760, deem it necessary to assert in America the primacy it had won in Britain, the colonists felt it a dangerous innovation, a fatal blow to the rights and powers they had received or through the years wrested from the king. The divergent views of the authority of Parliament held by the British and Americans proved to be irreconcilable, and in the end Parliamentary sovereignty was the rock on which the old empire split.

In any event, royal government, as has been suggested, became the norm for the British colonies in America in the eighteenth century. The king's main agent in the royal colonies was the governor. Appointed by the king and serving at his pleasure, the royal governor was to exercise the king's prerogative within the colony and to defend the king's rightful powers against any encroachment from his loyal subjects there. The governor was endowed with such power and responsibility, as the "Instructions" the king gave him at the time of his appointment made clear, to permit him to enforce Britain's colonial policy, particularly her commercial regulations.

The governor was to be aided in his colony by an advisory council, also appointed by the king, and by various royal officials in the provincial government, such officials as the colonial treasurer, the chief justice, the attorney general, the surveyor general, and the like. To assure the governor ample power to carry out his assigned mission, his instructions listed a number of specific areas of public business which he should control. The instructions specified among other things that the governor, alone or in conjunction with his council, should command the military forces of his province, conduct Indian affairs, dispose of public lands, expend public moneys and audit public accounts, appoint a number of public officials, suspend royal officials when necessary, and serve as the highest provincial court. And he and his council were to compose two of the three branches of the colonial legislature. In this last lay the source of his greatest strength and gravest weakness. Endowed with a double veto over the actions of the elected branch of the legislature, the governor and council, it would seem, could and for a long time did dominate the colonial legislatures. But the presence in the colonial legislature of an elective house meant that sooner or later the governor had to secure the cooperation of the colonists if he were in truth to govern. This proved to be his undoing. The main thrust of colonial politics in the eighteenth century was the rise of the elected houses to a position of dominance in the American legislatures, with a concomitant drastic curtailment, in fact if not in theory, of the king's prerogative as exercised by his provincial governors.

The British, however, did not rely solely on the governor and council to hold the elected assembly in check. They had a second line of defense against any colonial legislation that had a tendency to weaken their hold on the colonies. All colonial legislation was to be submitted to the King-in-Council for approval; any act of a colonial legislature which impinged upon royal authority in America or upon the operation of Britain's commercial system was not to go into effect until approved in London. The colonial assemblies tried various dodges and strategems to get around the effect of the king's review of their legislation, but royal disallowance of acts of the colonial legislatures proved a highly useful device for holding the colonies somewhat in check.

By 1700, the forms and procedures of colonial government and imperial administration were more or less set and all but one of the thirteen continental colonies that rebelled in 1776 were in existence and going concerns. The twelve colonies had surprisingly little in common besides their seventeenth-century beginnings. Most were established by Englishmen of one sort or another, but New York began as Dutch. Most of the colonists themselves were English, but even before the great non-English migration of the eighteenth century there were scattered through the colonies Germans, French, Dutch, Scots-Irish and Africans, as well as a smattering of Swedes, Poles, and Italians. The men who founded Virginia and Massachusetts, Carolina and Pennsylvania, Maryland and Rhode Island, acted from widely different motives and set for their colonies distinctly different goals, with marked effect. The peculiar genius of a founding father like Plymouth's William Bradford, Massachusetts' John Winthrop, Rhode Island's Roger Williams, or Pennsylvania's William Penn placed its own imprint upon the societies that emerged under these men's direction. Regional differences are not all born of climate and geography. Supervision by the English government, which might have provided a common denominator but did not, was one thing in the semiautonomous chartered and proprietary colonies and another in the royal colonies where British officials participated actively and extensively in colonial government. And at any given time the various colonies were in different stages of development. In social, political, and economic organization not only was venerable Massachusetts far in advance of younger colonies still raw frontiers in 1700, but so was

Pennsylvania, the youngest of them all. Established in unlike places at different times, under different circumstances, and for different purposes, the English colonies in North America were each from the start destined for a distinct, if not unique, pattern of development.

Nor did the circumstances and necessities of life in the American wilderness have the effect of reducing these disparate communities to a common mold. It is true that no matter when or why they came, or where they settled, the first contingents of colony builders had to clear land, erect shelters to house families, and raise crops for sustenance. If their venture was to achieve its purposes, whatever these might be, they also had to find outlets for the products of their labor in order to lift their community above the bare subsistence level. And they had to organize their society in such a way as to provide a tolerable degree of security for life and property. But the geography of the North American coast, the great variations in climate, soil, and the shape of the coastline, dictated varying solutions to the common problems of survival and economic progress.

One consequence of this accommodation to the dictates of geography by the first settlers became evident very early. From the start it was clear that the economic life of Massachusetts was to be very unlike that of Virginia and Maryland. But as the seventeenth century progressed the diverging economies of the various mainland colonies served less to accentuate individual differences between one colony and another than to divide them into three regional groupings: New England, the middle colonies, and the southern colonies, each with its characteristic economic pattern distinct from the other two.

The settlers of New England first found economic salvation in fishing and small-scale farming. With these forming a permanent base, Massachusetts-Bay and her progeny reached for prosperity through trade with the outside, notably with the West Indies. The southern colonies, on the other hand, very early came to rest their economy upon staple crops raised for the British market. It was clearly less the Puritan ethic than climate which ordained that New Englanders would forgo the cultivation of tobacco and rice with slave labor and turn instead to trade. The evolving economies of seventeenth-century New England and the southern colonies—and the more mixed economies of the middle colonies as well—opened up for seventeenth-century Americans very different roads to economic well-being, introducing sectional differences that went far beyond a mere difference in the way men sought to sustain their families or to make their fortunes. Only after the Americans began to struggle to form and then maintain their own union of states late in the eighteenth century did sectional rivalries and animosities develop to the point of giving rise to a strong sense of sectional identity; but many of the habits, attitudes, and institutions—plantation slavery being only the most obvious and important—which the Americans of the new nation were to discover to be peculiar to one section or another, had their roots in the seventeenth century.

In view of the wide range of differences among the individual colonies and the complexity of exploiting the economic potential of a sparsely populated region extending from the West Indies to Maine, it is small wonder that the men in London had their difficulties in giving proper coherence to the empire. It is hardly more surprising that they met with less than complete success. The Americans themselves were to stumble and almost fall on the block of state particularism when creating their republic, and they were to see that republic almost destroyed when put to the test by sectionalism in the nineteenth century. It also becomes understandable why the student of colonial America is hard put to make any general statement that applies to all of English America at a given time in the seventeenth century. This is the reason that a coherent and consecutive narrative encompassing the whole American story from the landing at Jamestown through the next century and one half is nowhere to be found.

For one who would understand something of seventeenth-century America, a detailed review of what is known of its history is the surest approach, and a rapid survey of the history of each individual colony is the most common. One alternative to either approach is to examine carefully the colonial experience of the two most important colonies, Massachusetts-Bay in New England and Virginia in the South. The two stages of development that these colonies passed through in the seventeenth century were sooner or later repeated in the other colonies. Every colony had to undergo the initial process of colonization as settlers came in, land was open up for cultivation, and institutions took form to provide a workable pattern of life. The first stage of colonial development may be said to have been completed when a colony reached the point at which its continued existence no longer remained in real doubt. As has been seen, the permanence of Virginia was not assured for perhaps a quarter of a century whereas Massachusetts-Bay was clearly on sound footing within a decade of the first landing. Much the same may be said of the later colonies of Carolina and Pennsylvania: the settlements in Carolina remained for decades small outposts struggling for survival, while in the space of a very few years William Penn succeeded in establishing a thriving colony. But sooner or later, each of the thirteen mainland colonies won its way through the first stage and began to function at a higher level.

This is not to say that Pennsylvania duplicated the earlier experience of Massachusetts, or that Carolina duplicated the earlier experience of Virginia. William Penn was not John Winthrop, Penn's Quakers were not Winthrop's Puritans, Charles II's England was not the England of Charles I, and by the 1670s America had traveled far from the days of William Bradford and Captain John Smith. The colonizers of Carolina and Pennsylvania had the benefit not only of the experience of the older colonies but of their existence as well. The proximity of Pennsylvania to settlements in Maryland and New York, and of Carolina to those in Virginia, greatly reduced the dangers of sudden extinction from the twin catastrophes: massacre by the Indians and starvation. The fact remains, however, that a general understanding of how the English colonies came into existence may be gained from a study of their prototypes in Virginia and Massachusetts. Taken together, the accounts of the establishment of these two colonies touch upon most of the basic ingredients of the colonizing process. Later English settlements in America began by acting out variations on themes clearly discernible in either early Massachusetts or early Virginia or in both.

The second stage of colonial development was reached in each colony when the settlers first began to take their existence in America for granted and to reach out with increasing assurance for the good things of life, for greater wealth, for the fulfillment of personal ambitions and the gratification of personal tastes, for the improvement of manners and morals, of houses and gardens, for more explicit yet broader definition of their rights as Englishmen, for a greater share of political power, but, above all else, for greater wealth. It was at this point that planters and merchants on the make ushered in a period of growth and expansion in the colony. Colonial society rapidly became more complex, both in its make-up and in its goals. And the colony itself became, in one way or another, a functioning part of England's commercial empire.

As long as the colony in its infancy had been utterly dependent on the English for support and protection, the settlers had been inclined to regard the English connection as almost wholly beneficent and beneficial. But their view of England's supervision subtly altered once the colony reached a position where its emergent merchants and planters could make a bid for a share, however small, of imperial wealth and power. The restrictions imposed on colonial trade by the Navigation Acts meant one thing to a man while he was struggling to eke out an existence on his newly cleared land and another thing to him after he began to aspire to engage in large-scale trade or commercial farming. Each colony first felt the full force of the English harness at precisely the moment it was undergoing the stresses and strains placed upon a compact and relatively primitive society by the expansion of its size and the dispersal of its people, and by the introduction of much greater diversification in wealth, status, occupation, and interests. Small wonder that in each colony the second stage of development was often marked by a series of crises and even by social convulsion like that of Bacon's Rebellion in Virginia in 1676.

A colony may be said to have passed through the second stage of its development and to have reached maturity once it had adjusted its social, political, economic, and religious arrangements to its own particular situation and had come to terms in one way or another with the fact of British supervision. If this be so, then it is clear that adolescence was over and done with in Massachusetts in the 1690s following the restoration of her charter; in Virginia not long after, certainly by the end of Spotswood's governorship in 1720, and in New York at about the same time; in South Carolina no later than the 1730s; in Georgia, begun and completed between the opening of the French and Indian War in 1754 and the repeal of the Stamp Act in 1766. Whatever the exact timing in these and the other colonies, in each there evolved a rather well-defined social structure, and its institutions, political and others, came to reflect with fair accuracy the realities of the social situation.

This transformation of colonial life was the work of people who were able to grasp and hold what the wilds of America offered. Energetic, tough, ruthless, unscrupulous perhaps, sometimes blessed with financial resources or backing in England, they mapped out the avenues to affluence in the colonies. With their newly won wealth, they established their social leadership and demanded, and gradually gained, a commensurate share of political power. This economic and social elite, asserting with increasing success its claim to political dominance through the elected assemblies of the legislatures, shaped the development of each colony in its third and, as it turned out, last stage of colonial development.

Chapter VI

Virginia and Massachusetts Come of Age

Virginia and Massachusetts suffered in the seventeenth century most of the growing pains endured sooner or later by the other colonies. Partly because of the hiatus of the English Civil War in the 1640s, neither Virginia nor Massachusetts was exposed to the pressures of English control when first emerging from the initial or outpost stage to the same degree that many of the later colonies were. But after 1660 each of them began the long and painful process of fitting itself into the evolving economic and political systems of the British Empire. The growth and expansion of the two colonies placed strains on the social fabric of each and produced dislocations in the body politic that required adjustment. And through it all entrepreneurs in trade and agriculture were laying the basis for the social, economic, and political dominance of merchants in eighteenth-century Massachusetts and of tobacco planters in eighteenth-century Virginia.

Given what the Massachusetts Puritans intended their New World colony to be and what it had in fact become by 1660, the leadership of Massachusetts had every reason to be alarmed at both the political and the economic implications of the colonial policy pursued by the Stuart rulers after the Restoration. The collapse of Puritan rule in England and the return to the throne of the son of the beheaded Charles I was in itself alarming. Nor was word of the new King's eagerness to conciliate Puritans in both old and new England sufficient to reassure those in Massachusetts.

Their suspicions, if not their worst fears, were confirmed soon enough when they learned the King's price for confirming the colony's charter of 1629. The government of Massachusetts was to acknowledge explicitly that the authority of the King extended to Massachusetts: by requiring of her officials an oath of allegiance to the King, by conducting all judicial processes in his name, and by repealing any colonial legislation in conflict with the laws of England. And it was to concede the right of English subjects in Massachusetts to practice the rites of the Church of England by permitting the use of the Book of Common Prayer and by no longer confining freemanship to members of the Puritan churches. The Puritan leaders of Massachusetts saw that to acknowledge the force of the royal prerogative in Massachusetts would be to open a fatal breach in that precious "independency" they had taken such pains to secure at the colony's inception and had guarded so jealously even against the claims of the Puritan Cromwell. The present demands to permit the Anglican form of worship were only omens of what was to come. Other measures tending to pervert their holy mission and subvert their holy commonwealth in America would surely follow.

The Massachusetts legislature, its general court, as it was called, considered Charles's demands but did nothing about them. Four years after coming to the throne, in 1664, Charles sent out commissioners to America to secure, among other things, the submission of Massachusetts on the King's terms. This failing, Charles then instructed the general court to send agents to England to discuss the impasse. The court refused. There the matter rested for ten years. The Great Plague, the burning of London, and the Dutch wars permitted the Puritan commonwealth in New England to enjoy its cherished isolation a few years longer.

Not all members of the general court had favored defiance of the King. A few among the sizable minority who wished for an accommodation with the King would have preferred royal rule to that of the local saints, but most were moderates who, while wishing to maintain a maximum of "independency of government," feared that to concede nothing would be to lose all. For the more devout Puritan leadership, such prudence was only a symptom of the falling away of zeal for the colony's true mission and further reason to stand firm whatever the consequences.

The profound sense of unease that had gripped the old Puritan leaders and in the 1660s stiffened their will to resist arose from something more than the threat the government of Charles II posed to their position. Thirty years in America had brought to pass much that was unexpected and unwished for. Massachusetts, once the advance guard of Christianity with the eyes of Protestantism upon her, sensed that the world had passed her by. For the English Puritan who had overthrown the monarchy and lived under the rule of Oliver Cromwell, New England Puritanism had lost much of its relevance and Winthrop's city on a hill had become a remote and near-forgotten village. English Puritans were even viewing with open impatience the refusal of Massachusetts to accept what they considered a generous offer from their common sovereign.

What was worse perhaps than the realization that the English Puritans no longer looked to the New World for the saving remnant, worse even than the painful recognition that there was a growing worldliness among the people of Massachusetts, was the knowledge that the New England churches, the very core of the Massachusetts experiment, were themselves in trouble. Instead of a widening band marching into the future, the body of saints was shrinking as the old settlers died one by one. After years of agonized soul searching, a synod of ministers meeting in 1662 acted to halt the erosion of the church rolls. Barred by their beliefs from admitting any to full membership except God's elect—those who could attest to their true conversion by an infusion of the Holy Spirit—the ministers voted to retain in a sort of associate membership the unredeemed descendants of the saints. This Halfway Covenant, as it was derisively called, opened the way for the church to hold the descendants of its members and then, as time passed, to take in any would-be true Christians.

Although the Halfway Covenant provided the Puritan churches with a way out of a blind alley and freed them to respond to the changing demands of the future, the necessity of devising it hardly strengthened confidence that Massachusetts could accept the intrusion of royal authority in the commonwealth without endangering the integrity of the Puritan experiment. Whether or not the colonists could in fact prevent the intrusion had not been put to the test fifteen years after the passage of the first Navigation Act of 1660, but by the mid-1670s England was in a position once again to turn its attention to the colonies. Charles created in 1674 a prestigious committee in his Privy Council to take charge of colonial affairs and in 1675 made the committee a royal commission. The Lords of Trade, as the members of the commission were called, took as their basic task the effective extension of royal authority to America. Their great object was to secure the enforcement of the acts of trade, and thereby make a reality of the economic system envisioned by Parliamentary legislation. A test of wills between King and colony had become inevitable.

The impact of the Navigation Acts on Massachusetts had been negligible before 1676, partly because New England's overseas trade already fit fairly well the pattern the acts sought to impose and partly because little had been done to enforce the acts. The flow of English goods to supply New England was "the stem from which the trade of Massachusetts branched." Lacking a staple for the English market, the New England merchants in order to pay for these goods had to find other outlets for the abundance of fish, food stuffs, and lumber products the region afforded. By the 1660s Boston merchants had developed extensive ties with English merchants and were deeply involved in supplying food and wood products to the Spanish and to the people in such places as Madeira, the West Indies, and Newfoundland. These traders were less concerned about the possible effects of the acts of trade than they were about the public policy of the Puritans who controlled the government of Massachusetts. Particularly alarming to the merchants was the prospect that the colony's recalcitrance would lead to the disruption of the network of trade they were weaving with the help of the English merchants.

The whole tendency of the Boston merchants' activity was to integrate Massachusetts in the emerging Atlantic economy, breaking down the walls of isolation upon which the Puritans had always relied to safeguard the Massachusetts experiment. Similarly, the main thrust of Restoration England's colonial policy as it affected Massachusetts was to reduce the isolation or autonomy of the colony. In effect, the merchants of Boston who dominated the New England economy and the men in London who were seeking to assert the rightful authority of the King throughout the empire were joining forces to threaten the Puritans' monopoly of political power in Massachusetts. The majority of the beleaguered Puritans who sat in the general court were determined to concede nothing. The government of Massachusetts had ignored the Navigation Acts in the past and would resist efforts to enforce them in the future, not because the largely rural membership of the general court wished to protect the interests of the colony's merchants but because it feared the consequences of conceding that an act of Parliament was binding on the people of Massachusetts.

What first involved the Lords of Trade in the affairs of Massachusetts were not the acts of trade, however. Deciding that the proprietary claims of Robert Mason and Ferdinando Gorges to Massachusetts-controlled New Hampshire and Maine should be heard at law, the Lords sent Edward Randolph to Boston in 1676. He was to look the situation over and order Massachusetts to send agents to London to defend her side in the Mason-Gorges case. Upon his return to England, Randolph reported to the Lords of Trade what he had observed in New England, focusing attention once again on the virtual independence of Massachusetts. Not only was the colony persisting in its refusal to acknowledge that the Navigation Acts applied to Massachusetts, it was also still not requiring an oath of allegiance to the King, not granting freedom of conscience to Anglicans, not permitting appeals to England from its courts, and not submitting legislation for review in London.

After considerable investigation, the Lords of Trade decided against launching an attack on Massachusetts' charter but made it clear that the colony was expected to conform to the King's longstanding instructions in all points at issue. The Massachusetts general court at its meeting in October 1677 immediately after King Philip's War, which had a traumatic effect on the colony, chose to regard the actions of the Lords of Trade as a victory for chartered rights instead of the temporary reprieve that it was. The legislature did go so far as to announce that it, not Parliament, would impose the trade regulations of the Navigation Acts, but it went no farther. The English government was quick to accept the challenge. In May 1678 the Lords of Trade recommended that *quo warranto* proceedings be instituted to vacate the Massachusetts charter. One month later Edward Randolph received a commission to be the first collector, surveyor, and receiver of the customs in New England. And in July the decision was reached to make New Hampshire a royal colony, an ominous development for the Massachusetts commonwealth. Just when all seemed lost, Titus Oates threw official England into a panic with his revelation of the supposed popish plot. A reconstituted Committee of Trade and Plantations decided that under the circumstances it would not be politically prudent to push its proceedings against the charter of the most conspicuous Puritan colony. Massachusetts suddenly had a second chance to find a way out.

The colony took advantage of this temporary lull in its struggle with the Lords of Trade to thwart Randolph in his determined efforts to enforce the Navigation Acts. It made no move to conciliate its critics in London. By 1681 the Lords of Trade were ready to force the issue with Massachusetts, and again the King ordered the colony to send agents to London. Upon receiving these orders, the general court met in special session. The scene was now set for the penultimate struggle between the two factions that had split Massachusetts politics since the Restoration.

On the one side were the moderates led by Governor Simon Bradstreet and on the other were the old-guard Puritans led by the deputy governor, Thomas Danforth. Bradstreet's moderates usually composed a majority of the assistants in the upper house of the legislature; the deputies of Danforth's so-called popular party always controlled the lower house. The moderates had the support of the economically powerful but politically frustrated merchants of Boston, some of whom had become out-and-out royalists. Devout Puritans, church members who dominated the electorate in the colony's towns, generally gave their allegiance to the popular cause. The position each held was clear enough. The moderates were convinced that unless at least minimal concessions were made to the Lords of Trade and the King, the colony was certain to lose its charter and with it everything they and their opponents wished to save. The popular party was equally convinced that the special mission of Massachusetts meant that to concede anything was to concede all, that it was better to go down to utter defeat than to bargain away their sacred heritage.

The bitter factional fight precipitated by the King's order to send agents to London was resolved only after a group of Boston ministers led by Increase Mather intervened and counseled the deputies to comply. They reluctantly agreed to appoint two agents. In the meantime it had become obvious that Randolph's hand was to be greatly strengthened in his enforcement of the Navigation Acts. To counteract this, the general court in 1682 itself enacted Parliament's Navigation Acts, thereby also affirming its contention that acts of Parliament did not extend to Massachusetts. It then set up machinery for enforcement, but only after the deputies made certain that they, and not the moderate governor, would control the appointment of the enforcement officials.

In early 1683, the Lords of Trade demanded that the general court's two agents, the moderate Joseph Dudley and Captain John Richards of the popular party, who had finally arrived in London, be authorized to amend the colony's charter. Failure to do this, they warned, would leave the Lords no alternative but to secure a writ to do away with the charter entirely. The general court was sufficiently alarmed to reverse itself and transfer to Randolph, the English official, the authority to enforce the Navigation Acts it had bestowed the year before upon its own appointees; but it refused to authorize its agents in London to accept alterations in the charter.

Again offered the choice of submitting to a revision of the charter or of having it revoked, the general court in the fall of 1683 engaged in a bitter and climactic debate. The deputies stood firm: Massachusetts would not compromise on the charter. On October 23, 1684, a judgment in chancery vacated the charter and the government of Massachusetts was legally dissolved.

The general court continued to govern Massachusetts and its two factions continued to bicker until May of 1686 when Edward Randolph arrived with a commission from the new king, James II, to erect a temporary government for Massachusetts, which would include Maine and New Hampshire. An appointed council composed largely of New Englanders, most of them merchants, took over the government of the enlarged colony under the leadership of Randolph. Randolph's vigorous and effective enforcement of the Navigation Acts did nothing to attach his fellow councilors to the new government, and their disenchantment became complete after Governor Edmund Andros arrived in December to set up the Dominion of New England.

Old factional differences in Massachusetts were soon buried in a common animosity for the lordly Andros who governed all New England, and eventually New York and New Jersey as well, with little reference to either the interests or feelings of the only men who might have been expected to support his regime—the members of the Dominion council and the community of merchants from which they were drawn. So it was that when news came in 1689 of the flight of James and the accession of the Protestant rulers, William and Mary, the revolt in Massachusetts against Andros and his minions was swift, virtually unopposed, and bloodless.

William III fully recognized the patent necessity of restoring the elected assemblies in the northern colonies; but neither he nor his advisers had any intention of handing Massachusetts back to the old Puritan establishment. After reviving the charters of Rhode Island and Connecticut and reinstituting royal government in New Hampshire, the King granted to Massachusetts a new, revised charter that went into effect in 1691. The charter guaranteed that there would be no return to the old isolation or to the former Puritan monopoly of power; the Puritans of Massachusetts hereafter would share the powers of colonial government with royal officials from the outside and with non-Puritans at home. Under the new charter, property holders in the colony, most of whom were artisans or farmers, elected the members of the lower house of the legislature. The assemblymen in turn chose the councilors who sat in the upper house. But the king henceforth appointed the governor and lieutenant governor, and the governor could reject if he chose any of the assembly's nominees for the council. Further guarantees of the presence and influence of royal authority within the bounds of the erstwhile Puritan commonwealth came in 1696 with the passage of a new navigation act and the creation of the Board of Trade, and the subsequent erection of vice-admiralty courts in the colonies.

The merchants' most important political asset derived from their close association with English merchants of wealth and influence. These crucial ties with London, made possible and necessary by their extensive trading activities, permitted the Massachusetts merchants to influence the choice of royal officials for the colony and hence to have a voice in the day-to-day decisions of these officials while in Massachusetts, including decisions relating to the enforcement of the Navigation Acts.

The merchants also established a political base within the colonial government. In the 1690s they gained control of the new provincial council and continued to dominate it for over a half century. The growing secularization and commercialization of Massachusetts made it easier for the colony's mercantile element to persuade the elected assembly to nominate merchants for seats on the council; the merchants' peculiar relationship with the appointed royal governors ordinarily made it possible for them to assure the rejection of any assembly nominees to the council who might threaten their control of what had become the merchants' political bailiwick. The point is that control of the council assured the merchants of participation in all colonial legislation and in many of the executive actions of the governor. With their wealth and prestige, their invaluable connections abroad, and their control of the council, the merchants were able to operate the Massachusetts political system pretty much to their liking until the 1760s when the intervention of Parliament threatened their hegemony, forcing the merchants to the forefront of a resistance movement that eventually led to the destruction of all their old arrangements.

Colonial Massachusetts was set both in structure and direction before the end of the seventeeth century. That is, the main elements of the colonial society that was to lead America into revolution in 1775-1776 were already discernible three quarters of a century before. If Massachusetts in 1700 was the child of Winthrop's Puritan commonwealth it was also the father of Sam Adams's independent republic. Massachusetts under the later Stuarts saw the relaxing of the hold both of Puritan leadership and of the Puritan ideal, opening the way for a radical readjustment of its economic and political, and even religious, institutions and for its integration into the British Empire of the eighteenth century. It is true that time and circumstance within Massachusetts itself were already bringing shifts and change to the colony well before the active intervention of the Lords of Trade in the 1670s, but it was the government in London that ultimately forced the issue in Boston and delivered the *coup de grace* to the old commonwealth. Periodic conflict between central and local authority has always been a constant of American politics. Here we have a classic example of central authority prevailing and imposing bitterly opposed changes of a fundamental sort. The British government did more in a century and a half to shape American life and institutions than the historian's recital of its fumbling and bumbling would suggest.

Colonial Virginia, too, was set in its structure and direction by the early eighteenth century. But the two colonies of Virginia and Massachusetts, different from the beginning, became studies in contrast as they matured. In Virginia, planters, not merchants, gained economic, social, and then political dominance. The planters' economic base was, of course, agriculture, not trade, and they in time developed their political base within colonial government in the lower house of the legislature, the elected house of burgesses, instead of in the council. The dependence of the local magnates upon the cultivation of tobacco fitted Virginia, in contrast to New England, into the classic mercantile mold as a colony that served the mother country by providing her with a marketable staple and a profitable outlet for goods and investment. Although the great planters of eighteenth-century Virginia had extensive connections in Britain, particularly with merchants in the tobacco trade who in effect underwrote the plantation system through credit advances to the colony's planters, they relied less upon the support of powerful friends in Britain for their political influence than the New Englanders did. In a society devoted almost exclusively to farming, the advantages they derived from large landholdings and numerous slaves were sufficient.

To be or become a great planter in a community of small ones was at the same time to develop and to demonstrate the appropriate qualities for political leadership in that community. The instruments for the planters' political control were immediately at hand in the decentralized religious and political establishments of this rural society. Who but successful planters in parish and county had the means, the time, training, the experience, prestige, or even the desire to conduct the public business, to sit on the vestry and on the county court? And in a homogeneous society such as this, who was there to suffer from, or object to, the planters' control of the vestry and the court or to consider any alternative to men drawn from the local oligarchy to represent the county in the legislature in faraway Williamsburg? After all, the great planter was a small planter writ large, and together they comprised the vast majority of the politically effective in the colony.

Unlike the Boston merchants, the Virginia planters in the eighteenth century did not have to manipulate their political system to reconcile clashing interests in the colony and to defend their primacy from the inroads of competing groups in colonial society. But, like the merchants, they had to cope with the fact that their power was circumscribed by royal officials and their interests vitally affected by British policies. Whereas the merchants strained to domesticate the royal officials in Massachusetts, the planters in Virginia concentrated upon reducing their influence. The Massachusetts leaders utilized the authority of royal officials to assure their own continued domination of colonial government and the promotion of their particular mercantile interests; the planters in the house of burgesses, for their part, whittled away at the authority of the royal governor and council with the happy knowledge that what the king lost of his prerogative in Virginia they, and they alone, would gain. Their undisputed dominance of colonial society and their unchallenged control of the organs of local government assured this. When the time came that Virginia and Massachusetts found themselves on the road leading to revolution, the Boston merchant-patriots were forced to resort to mob violence to clear the way by isolating and intimidating their erstwhile allies, the royal officials in their midst, whereas Virginia's leaders had to do little more than reach an agreement among themselves about the route the colony should follow and the speed it should travel.

Until the crisis of the 1760s the Boston merchants were content for the most part to use their political influence to govern the colony, attempting few legislative innovations beyond various stratagems to increase the chronically short supply of circulating currency. But the Virginians did not leave their plantations and take a seat in the house of burgesses to manage a successful enterprise like that of New England commerce. Rather, they went to Williamsburg to deal with intractable, interrelated, and still familiar problems that beset those who stake their fortunes on the production of a staple crop for the world market. Undercapitalization, fluctuating commodity prices, an unfavorable balance of trade, shortage of credit and currency, and an enforced labor system, all leading to growing planter indebtedness and shrinking room for maneuver, prompted incessant legislative tinkering to halt the upward spiral of debt. Nearly any move the burgesses might make to reduce the colony's dependence on tobacco, the slave trade, and British credit was certain to arouse formidable opposition from British merchants with heavy investments in the tobacco and slave trades.

It is not surprising, then, that a diversified economy freed of the domination of British merchants should be the long-range goal of Virginia's farsighted leaders from the early seventeenth century to the outbreak of the Revolution. In the 1660s Governor William Berkeley made a concerted effort to change the direction of the colony's economic development just as the plantation system was taking on the characteristics that made it the glory and the bane of eighteenth-century Virginia. Berkeley, who had been the king's governor in Virginia from 1641 until the colony reluctantly and perforce gave Cromwell its allegiance in 1652, returned to his old post at the invitation of the council and burgesses even before Charles's restoration in 1660. Exceedingly well connected in court circles and himself first among the planters hard at work establishing a landed gentry along the banks of Virginia's rivers, Berkeley had high hopes and great plans for the Old Dominion when he went to London shortly after the Restoration to seek concessions for his colony from the new King.

Berkeley was not displeased that the King and Parliament had at last stepped in to direct the development of the mercantile empire. He was convinced, however, that the recent Navigation Act of 1660 was a false start. The wealth and future greatness of the empire lay not in restricting colonial development to the confines of the immediate interests of selfish English merchants, as the Navigation Act tended to do, but rather in developing for the enrichment of all the limitless potential of English America, of which Virginia was the crowning jewel.

Berkeley was back in Virginia by early 1663 to try his hand at developing and diversifying Virginia's economy, with a promise of greater freedom of action for his government than he could have dared hoped. The rub was that he had to work within the limitations of the Navigation Acts and, even more important, could not look to the royal treasury for the funds required to initiate the ambitious and costly economic program he envisioned. There was nothing for it but to extract through taxation from the already desperately hard-pressed colonists enough at least to make a beginning.

For a decade Governor Berkeley did what he could to encourage the production of such things as hemp, flax, and silk and to build towns. Both the urgency and the difficulty of achieving what he sought to do were intensified by the sad state of the tobacco trade. Despite all the Governor's efforts, tobacco remained a glut on the market and prices for the weed remained disastrously low, a circumstance that hardly increased the colonists' ability or their will to finance Berkeley's projects, or lessened the importance of their doing so. The reward for his unremitting efforts, and the price he paid for his failure, was rebellion in the colony.

Governor Berkeley was neither the first nor the last political leader to meet with disaster in pushing an impoverished people to accept deeper deprivations in return for the prospect of future gain. The trouble started when a number of white colonists in 1675-1676 launched a savage and unauthorized campaign against nearby Indians. Frightened by reports of King Philip's War in New England and filled with a long-standing hatred for Indians and a hunger for Indian land, lesser and would-be planters rejected in an outburst of violence the policy of the old governor and his council of stabilizing the boundaries between the settlers and the Indians. By 1676 the assault on the Indians had turned into a full-scale revolt against Berkeley's rule led by the fiery young Nathaniel Bacon, a recent arrival from England.

At the meeting of the general assembly in June 1676 the disaffected planters in the house of burgesses revealed the depths of their resentment in having been cut off from political influence and office by the Berkeley regime. The laws the June assembly enacted reflected the burgesses' determination to break the political and social monopoly enjoyed by the Governor and his Green Spring faction of greater planters who filled his council and held most of the more lucrative and important offices.

The burgesses under Bacon's banner derived mass support for

the rebellion from ordinary farmers. These farmers, who formed the great majority of settlers, shared the anti-Berkeley planters' frustration at the economic plight of the colony though not their concern for broadening the base of planter leadership in colonial society and government. The small farmers were apparently disturbed by growing evidence of the emergence of the planters as a new social class. To be outstripped in a common pursuit by one's neighbor and to observe him assume pretensions to a higher station in life does not breed satisfaction with one's own lot. Nor were the small farmers likely to view with equanimity the process by which the planters were consolidating their control in the counties through their domination of the vestries and county courts. The day would come when planter leadership would be accepted seemingly as a matter of course, but for the present the price lesser men exacted for supporting the rebellious planters was laws from the June assembly designed to restrict planter control at the county level.

Determined to push the war against the Indians, the June assembly forced Governor Berkeley to accept Bacon as commander in chief of the colony's armed forces. Berkeley soon found his position in Jamestown untenable and fled to Virginia's eastern shore. There he raised a force of 300 men and in September returned to Jamestown. A series of confused and half-hearted skirmishes between Berkeley's supporters and Bacon's settled nothing. But in October Bacon died, and the tide abruptly turned. When three royal commissioners arrived from London in early 1677 with a detachment of troops to restore order, they discovered that the embittered old governor was in complete control, after having stamped out the rebellion and hanged a number of its leaders.

Government by a resident planter had failed. The experiment in wide autonomy for Virginia had failed. Bacon's rebellion undoubtedly made a reversal of England's Virginia policy inevitable, but a move to tighten control over the colony was in line with the thinking of the Lords of Trade in the late 1670s as they tinkered with the machinery of empire and increased the pressure on the recalcitrant saints in Massachusetts. The movement toward centralization was also congenial to the notions of Charles in the later years of his reign and even more so to those of his brother James after he

became King in 1685. Charles and then James in the 1680s sent out
Stuart courtiers, men like Thomas Lord Culpeper and Francis Lord
Howard of Effingham, to govern Virginia and to govern it with as
little consultation with the local planters as they could manage. Rule
by lordly outsiders had the predictable effect of creating an unprecedented unity among the local planters, new and old, large and
small. Deprived of their privileged position in the governor's inner
circle, many of the great planters of Berkeley's Green Spring faction now joined forces with those who had sought their overthrow
in the recent rebellion. The governor could still generally command the support of the great planters holding office on his council
but not with the same certainty that Berkeley once could.

Although Virginia's elected assembly in the 1680s did not suffer
the fate of those in New England under Andros's Dominion, the
house of burgesses continued to play second fiddle, if a noisy one,
to both governor and council. Most significant for the future of the
burgesses was the split that developed between great planters like
Philip Ludwell and the governor, leading ultimately to an alliance
between great planters and lesser ones in the general assembly to
resist outside control. In this lay the basis for the political hegemony
of the local planters in the eighteenth century and for the ultimate
domination of colonial government by the house of burgesses. But
for the moment things were going the governor's way. Culpeper,
and Effingham in particular, had considerable success in maintaining royal authority in the colony, and even in extending it at the
expense of the colonial general assembly.

Any drift toward centralization and government by prerogative
was abruptly checked, however, by the revolution in England in
1688. The Virginia governors continued in the years that followed
to uphold royal power in the Old Dominion and to resist encroachment by the council and burgesses on the king's prerogative, but
the assertion of royal authority was no longer an end in itself as it
had been in the 1680s. The measure of Governor Francis Nicholson's success in the 1690s and again in the early eighteenth century,
for example, was not how strictly he limited colonial participation
in government but rather how effectively he used the royal authority at his disposal to protect and promote English mercantile
interests in the colony. The British thrust toward the professionali-

zation and rationalization of colonial administration was perhaps greater during the reigns of William and Anne than at any other time until after the French and Indian War. Given the structure of colonial government, the crux of the matter for the new-style royal governors in Virginia was the proper management of the colony's legislature.

For nearly two decades after 1690 it was the assemblage of great planters in the Virginia council, led by Commissary James Blair, who required the governor's deftest handling. These men stood at the apex of Virginia society and composed one of the three branches of the legislature. They were also royal officials. As members of the governor's council, and incumbents in most of the appointive offices, they held their commissions from the king and shared in the governor's exercise of executive powers. Their preeminent position in Virginia gave great weight to their opinion in all aspects of colonial affairs and permitted them to exert considerable if not decisive influence in London in such matters as the king's choice of councilors for the colony or even of a new governor. To get around opposition from the grandees of the council, the two ablest governors of the period, Nicholson and Alexander Spotswood, were apt to assume the guise of defenders of the common people against the threat of oligarchic rule. But for the governor to court the people and their representatives in the house of burgesses in order to undermine the appointive council bore its own peculiar dangers: it was the house, not the council, that was in the end to be the governor's undoing.

Until his final departure from Virginia in 1705 Governor Nicholson had remarkable success in dealing with the burgesses, although he earned the undying enmity of commissary Blair and of most of the council. Similarly, Governor Spotswood after his arrival in 1710 enjoyed good relations with the house for several years, and he met with only sporadic opposition from the entrenched council. The burgesses' cooperative attitude reflected wide popular support for a number of constructive but perhaps overly ambitious measures advocated by the ebullient governor. When, after about five years, Spotswood's efforts at extensive reforms—in public land policy, the regulation of the Indian trade and the tobacco trade, the conduct of Indian affairs, and the colony's arrangements for its defense—had not fulfilled expectations, the burgesses broke with the governor and joined forces to checkmate Spotswood and redirect public policy. The house then proceeded to demonstrate that it had come into its own, that it could deal on equal terms with the governor—and with the council. Within a decade of Spotswood's resignation in 1722, the house of burgesses had become the dominant element in colonial government.

The shift of power to the house of burgesses in the generation following the Revolution of 1688 reveals a great deal about Britain's phenomenal success in administering her eighteenth-century empire before 1754 and about the cruel dilemma she faced after 1763. The representative principle that had found its diverse ways into the colonial constitution and there become firmly embedded by 1700 allowed the constitution to respond with unwonted promptness and precision to changes in the complexion of colonial society. The rise of the house of burgesses coincided with the maturing of Virginia's plantation system and of the planter class it spawned. The recovery of the tobacco market in the 1680s after Bacon's Rebellion did not mark the end of its ups and downs, for cycles of prosperity and hard times remained characteristic of the Virginia economy until the Revolution and afterward; but it did usher in an era of rapid and virtually continuous economic growth. Planters, the large-scale commercial farmers, expanded their operations, and many others joined their ranks. They opened up the piedmont and bought thousands upon thousands of Africans to work their fields. Self-confident and secure, ambitious, experienced, and in firm control of the levers of power in the locality where they lived, they found in the house of burgesses a ready instrument to protect and advance their interests.

In the late seventeenth century, then, Virginia and Massachusetts each passed through a period of disorder and instability as dynamic elements in their societies—planters in Virginia and merchants in Massachusetts—emerged and claimed a proximate share of power, whether at the expense of older elements in colonial society or of the royal prerogative, or of both. The resulting redistribution of power and rearrangement of institutions reflecting the realities of the social situation created the context for orderly expansion and growth in the eighteenth century.

A detailed study of variations on this process in other colonies would be equally instructive were it not for the extraordinary importance of Virginia and Massachusetts in eighteenth-century America. In South Carolina, for instance, it was the rice planter and his fellow planter-merchant of Charleston who pushed to the forefront, overthrew proprietary government in 1719, and under the royal governor, Thomas Johnson, in the 1730s made the colonial house of assembly the political expression of their dominance of Carolina society. The planter aristocracy that emerged in South Carolina was not only unlike that of Virginia but also exerted its political influence in a very different way. The culture of rice was limited to the banks of Carolina's tidal streams; it required a large investment of capital and labor; and it was marketed abroad in a way quite unlike the way tobacco was marketed. And Charleston developed as the one port through which all of the colony's trade was funneled, making it a genuine urban center. The consequence of all this was that the planter aristocracy in South Carolina was much smaller, individually wealthier, and more concentrated in area than was the tobacco aristocracy of Virginia. The wealthy Carolina planters and merchants, all living in and about Charleston, moved directly into colonial government and ruled from the center without the intervention of local organs of government, whereas the Virginia planters on their scattered plantations developed and secured control of local government and, from their county fiefdoms, periodically sent emissaries to the house of burgesses. This dispersal, or localization, of political authority in Virginia nurtured political talent in the eighteenth century far more successfully than did Carolina's centralization of authority, and in the nineteenth century it made for much greater political stability and restraint.

And there were the colonies of Pennsylvania and New York, each rivaling Massachusetts and Virginia in importance before the end of the colonial period. Philadelphia merchants were like Boston merchants and New York merchants, and unlike both. The deLanceys and Livingstons on their landed estates in New York had much in common with the Carters and Byrds of Virginia and the Rutledges and Pinckneys of South Carolina, but a manor on the Hudson was not a tobacco plantation on the James or rice fields on the Ashley. Discernible in each of these colonies, and in the others as well, are variations on many of the same political institutions, social patterns, and economic arrangements. No two were ever identical, however; and the mix was always different enough to set apart any colony from her twelve sister colonies.

Chapter VII

Colonial Growth and Expansion

The history of colonial America can be told largely in terms of how European immigrants sought and found solutions to problems posed by life in the New World. Perhaps the grandest example of the European assault on the American wilderness, and certainly one of the most lasting in its effects on the American character, was the Puritan attempt to create a godly community on the shores of Massachusetts Bay. But even the early Puritans were much of the time of necessity concerned with more mundane things. Like settlers before and after them, they had to find ways to secure food and shelter, and they had to arrange their affairs in a way that made for their common peace and safety.

In working out the patterns of their existence the Puritans and other colonists came up against a factor missing in the European equation. The seemingly endless stretches of unused land on the American continent altered old rules and promised new answers. To get this land into the hands of those who would use it and to guarantee to them the right of its use and the fruits of its cultivation was itself an arduous enough task, and one of paramount importance. Where the rich and plentiful soil of America had its profoundest effect, however, was in the gradual accommodation of the settlers' thinking, their view of themselves and of the world, to the emerging fact that no man need be fixed in status or forever frozen in poverty. Year in and year out during a century and a half, and well before the industrial revolution had turned Europe topsy-turvy, the American colonists were living in a corner of the earth where the abundance of resources permitted a man to rise or fall by his own efforts with relative ease. It was a new world.

During the seventeenth century, the English settlers in America, as we have seen, faced and dealt with most of the basic problems of transplanting old patterns and institutions and of gradually devising new ones, in government, religion, economics, social arrangements, and imperial relationships. There were problems yet to be faced in 1700 and solutions yet to be reached, but the problems of the eighteenth century were generally of a different sort, more complex, more interrelated, less soluble. This was so not only because much had transpired in the seventeenth century, to which the eighteenth was heir, but also because of the sheer growth of colonial America in the eighteenth century. Growth in numbers, wealth, production, area, variety, and complexity transformed the American scene and radically altered the basic terms in which men functioned. The explosive growth of the colonies was both cause and consequence of the maturing of colonial society, which in turn made the Revolution of 1776 possible, some would say inevitable, and did much to make it the kind of revolution it was.

What Americans experienced in the eighteenth century was not simply a growth in scale but a growth in kind as well. Bare statistics do not fully convey the scale of growth, much less its implications. To say, for instance, that between 1700 and 1775 the colonial population grew from 1 to 3 million conveys less perhaps than to say that its relative increase was that of a people of 200 million becoming a people of 600 million. And the fact that this increase in population owed little to English and much to non-English immigration as well as to natural increase further complicates the problem. How did the influx of thousands upon thousands of German pietists and land-hungry Scots-Irish Presbyterians affect American patterns and attitudes other than by swelling the number of inhabitants? And what of the sudden majority of American-born for whom Europe was not even a dim memory? But the thing that the raw statistics of colonial population most profoundly conceals is the impact of the hundreds of thousands of blacks—by 1776 there were about 600,000 living in continental North America, most but by no means all in the southern colonies—who were forcibly transported from Africa to the New World to be held in bondage. The consequences of the massive shift in the plantation colonies from white indentured servants to African slaves beginning late in the seventeenth century were, of course, for then and now incalculably great.

The ready supply of land in America, combined with the continuing if neither steady nor always adequate flow of British capital to the colonies in the form of credit advances, assured that population growth would have an immediate and profound impact on the colonial economy. Every substantial increase in the number of inhabitants, slave or free, meant an expanded area of settlement and an increase in the total value of produce from colonial farm and plantation and of colonial trade on the high seas. The consequent increase in total wealth introduced into every colony wider disparities in incomes, for a disproportionate share of the wealth being generated by commercial farming and trade quite naturally flowed into the hands of those managing these enterprises, the planters and the merchants.

The eighteenth century, then, brought to America a much wider differentiation in men's wealth or condition, function, and status. There was no real social stratification in the European sense, however—aside from slavery. In fact, because economic opportunities were far greater than in the early years of settlement, social mobility or fluidity in the English colonies may have been more pronounced than it had been in the less differentiated, and consequently in a sense more egalitarian, society of the seventeenth century. The effect of all this social and economic change upon manners and mores, living conditions, political ideas and practices, religious views and organizations, Anglo-American relations both cultural and institutional, town life, popular attitudes and aspirations— upon, in short, the character of American life and thought—was, of course, profound. It is the proper object of investigation for one who would have some knowledge and understanding of America in the first half of the eighteenth century.

The rapid expansion of black slave labor in the eighteenth century best reveals something of the scale, ramifications, and lasting

consequences of the explosive growth of Britain's thirteen mainland colonies after 1700. Here we have, too, the genesis of all the
tragedy and irony that have characterized the relations between
whites and blacks in the North American colonies and states. Although the first African servants were brought to Jamestown as
early as 1619 and seventeenth-century Virginians and Marylanders
must take the credit, or bear the onus, for having given legal
definition to the institution of American slavery, it was not until the
1690s that the southern colonists were in a position to utilize Negro
slaves in large numbers. There followed a century of often frenzied
importation of slaves from Africa and the West Indies, first mostly
into the Chesapeake colonies and subsequently largely into
Carolina and Georgia. Virginia, for example, which had fewer than
3000 slaves in 1680 and hardly 6000 in 1700, imported 5000
blacks in 1727 alone. The vast majority of Negroes brought to what
is now the United States arrived between 1700 and 1775. And
almost all were brought by slave traders operating out of Britain or
New England. It is overstating the case, but not by much, to say that
Rhode Island became nearly as dependent on the slave trade as
Maryland and Virginia were dependent on slave labor.

The introduction of a large number of black slaves produced
after the turn of the century a spectacular and immediate expansion
of tobacco production and of the tobacco trade in the Chesapeake
colonies. Hardworking farmers in Maryland and Virginia exploited
the land and the now-plentiful labor supply to create the great
tobacco plantations of the eighteenth century. A powerful planter
class rapidly reached maturity, putting its stamp on eighteenth-
century Virginia and thereafter on the new nation its leaders did
so much to establish. The rewards for success in this planter society,
which became the general pattern for all the southern colonies,
were the enjoyment of many of the niceties and much of the substance of European civilization. Well-to-do tobacco and rice planters built fine houses, fitted them with handsome furnishings, found
the leisure to visit and be visited, to entertain and be entertained,
sometimes traveled home to England and often sent their sons there
to be educated. Horse racing, cockfighting, theatricals, musicales,
and balls broke the monotony of plantation life in Virginia and
enlivened the scene in Charleston where the Carolina rice planters

gathered. The rigors of carving out a niche in the primeval forests gave way to the pleasures and amenities of life in country seats and town houses.

These eighteenth-century planters of Maryland and Virginia and of Carolina were no favored aristocrats living off the fat of the land, however. They were men of business who acquired land and purchased labor and then exploited both to create wealth. A plantation did not appear of itself or turn a profit without careful management and close application. Only a relatively few colonists became large planters, and, as useful as they were, neither family connections nor a good inheritance assured a man a permanent place among the local elite. The ultimate price of failure among these commercial farmers was the sure loss of status.

The thing that makes this planter aristocracy in a colonial society worthy of more than passing notice is that it gave to the future the paradoxical heritage of remarkable political management and a labor system based upon race and enforced servitude. The Virginia planters developed the capacity, the will, and the necessary mastery of political technique to govern the colony in conjunction with royal officials and to govern it well. Nor was the government they provided merely effective; it was also to a considerable degree enlightened. Like the rest of the colonial elite, Virginia's leaders absorbed in the eighteenth century the liberal political tradition passed down from the radicalism of England's seventeenth-century Puritan Commonwealth. Government by consent, constitutional limitations on the exercise of power, a balanced constitution, the inviolability of man's reserved rights were not mere slogans to colonial practitioners of politics. Harrington, Sidney, Locke, Milton and Marvel became for the more knowledgeable among them expositors of the glorious constitution of Britain which the colonists shared, and English publicists from Trenchard and Gordon to Price and Priestley its admirable watchdogs. The Virginia planters' concern for individual liberty and local rights was genuine, and their awareness of the role they played as burgesses in defending such rights and liberties was acute. The first half of the eighteenth century gave remarkable preparation both in providing political experience and in inculcating political ideas to those men in Virginia and elsewhere who were to carry through a revolution to preserve and widen human liberty.

But at what price this political acumen and political idealism? It was only with a heightened realization in the years immediately preceding the Revolution of how precarious and how precious human liberty was that Americans began dimly to see that the liberty they cherished had been bought in part at the cost of its total loss by the Africans in their midst. Slavery's patent violation of the Revolution's credo of freedom and equality hastened its abolition in those newly independent states where slaves were relatively few and of no great economic importance; but when viewing the hordes of blacks working the southern plantations the best most of the founding fathers could do was to label slavery an evil and wish it away. However grievous a wrong or blatant a contradiction they felt slavery to be, few could envision extending to the black man the freedom and equality they had claimed for themselves. This remained for other men in other centuries to attempt.

The shipment of slaves to the mainland of North America increased dramatically in the years after 1698 when Parliament withdrew the Royal African Company's monopoly of the slave trade and opened it up to all traders. By this time, the institution of slavery as practiced, with minor variations, in continental British America was already fairly well fixed in Virginia and Maryland. Through the years, Negro slavery had been gradually defined by custom and given legal sanction by successive acts of the legislatures of the two colonies. South Carolina, for its part, initially followed the lead of Barbados in its approach to slavery. By 1740, however, slavery in Carolina was virtually indistinguishable from that found in Virginia, except that the extremely high ratio of blacks to whites in the low country led to stricter enforcement of the codes regulating the conduct of slaves in Carolina and life for the slaves was more miserable, and very often shorter, in the Carolina rice swamps than on the Virginia tobacco plantations.

All slaves wherever they labored were nonwhite—Negroes, mulattoes, and fewer and fewer Indians. They were property to be bought and sold at will. And they and all their progeny born of slave women were forever to remain bondsmen unless set free by their owners. As property, they did not share the civil and political rights freemen enjoyed or might in the future win. To assure their submission, colonial legislatures rigidly restricted the slaves' movement and right of assemblage. The legislatures set and the courts imposed on the slaves special and, even for the times, extraordinarily harsh penalties for all the crimes men are prone to. Laws against miscegenation combined with laws making the children of a slave mother the property of her owner went as far as could be to assure endless generations of black bondsmen working in the fields of white masters.

The cost of enslavement to the uprooted Africans in sorrow and suffering is beyond reckoning. Denied all opportunities to share in the American bonanza they were helping to create, slaves could expect for themselves and their descendants only a bare subsistence in return for unending toil. But worst of all, or so the generality of men have come to believe, was the degradation of the human spirit flowing from a man's being the property, very like an ox or an ass, of another man. This was the brute fact of American slavery as it emerged in the seventeenth century and was practiced in the eighteenth and nineteenth centuries. No amount of masterly compassion or servile docility could disguise that fact.

And yet this is not the end of it. The hook in American slavery that dug deepest and held longest was the restriction of slave status to persons of color. Well before the eighteenth century was over, white Americans were recognizing that slavery was something more than a profitable economic institution: it had become, if indeed it was not almost from its beginnings, a system of social control, a comprehensive device for keeping the Negro separate and inferior to the white man. This marriage of slavery and race, of economic interest and racial prejudice, was what made the problem of slavery so extraordinarily complex in North America—made slavery "necessary" for the whites, and made it peculiarly "evil"— and was to make its abolition so long in coming and so bloody when it came. And it has meant prolonging the effects of slavery. Racial antipathy, whether the child of slavery or father to it, fixed upon the legally free Negro for generations the badge of his former servitude.

That slavery as practiced in the British colonies of North America built up massive psychological and material difficulties for the black in his ultimate day of freedom is indisputable. But what of the white men who relied upon slavery to fashion the vigorous and politically creative society of eighteenth-century America? For the full effect upon white America of the fear, guilt, greed, pride, arrogance, and taste for power bred of slavery, one must look to the America of the nineteenth century and beyond. Or for a telling clue he might simply look at the words often used after 1800 to assert the positive virtues of human slavery or of racial control.

One of the earliest and most enduring arguments advanced to justify slavery in the colonies was that by his enslavement the African was rescued from heathenism and given hope for his salvation through the grace of the Christian God. The church with its teaching of Christian humility and its promise of an afterlife also did much to bolster slavery by reconciling the pious slave to his lot. In fact, there was hardly an institution that took root in seventeenth-century America which did not owe its existence in part to the support and nurture religion gave it. The family, the town, education, government itself, all relied heavily upon organized religion and religious belief to hold their own against the disruptive forces of isolation, alienation, and constant change in a strange, crude land.

New World settlers were quite conscious of the crucial role Christian churches must play in their venture not only if they were to retain any hope of salvation but also if they were to prevent a gradual reversion to barbarism in the wilds of North America. Whatever their beliefs about the relationship of church and state, the early settlers in America did not hesitate to use the full force of the state to support religion and its dictates relating to morals and conduct. People striking out from Europe or from established areas in the colonies to seek new homes time and again turned to religious doctrine for the undertaking's rallying point and to fellow churchmen for its composition. Once settled, they looked to the church to give their nascent community a measure of coherence. The fervor with which frontiersmen down through the years responded to the stimuli of evangelical preaching in successive "Awakenings" underlines not only the emotional need for religious experience felt by uprooted Americans but also their intuitive recognition that by coming together in worship they were moving toward the re-creation of something not unlike the settled life they had left behind.

In a sense, the church simply repeated on the advancing American frontier the role it had played in Winthrop's Boston and in Jamestown. For three centuries it continued to serve as an indispensable civilizing agent and a giver of a sense of continuity and community to Americans on the move. On the other hand, there emerged from the American experience and condition a broad and distinctive approach to organized religion. This happened in the eighteenth century, not the seventeenth. The expansion and growth of the colonies after 1700 had a profound impact on the religious arrangements and attitudes of eighteenth-century America and led to the general acceptance of new working principles about the proper relationship of organized religion to individuals, to society, and to the state, and about the relationship one to another of the multiplying sects or denominations that came to compose the American religious establishment.

For one thing, the changes in colonial society in the eighteenth century resulting from material growth made it a practical necessity for a colony to tolerate the exercise of differing forms of worship within its bounds. This by no means had been generally the case in the seventeenth century. The Massachusetts Puritans had not welcomed the unorthodox, and Virginia had as a matter of course established Anglicanism as the only form of worship for its inhabitants. It is true that in the early days the Dutch West India Company had extended the religious toleration practiced by the Dutch to New Amsterdam and that the Duke of York confirmed this practice after he took over in 1664, but for long religious toleration in New York meant little more than neglect of religion to the distress of its inhabitants. It is also true that William Penn in 1682 decreed the toleration of all Protestants in Pennsylvania in order to provide a secure haven for his coreligionists among the Society of Friends and to attract to his colony the industrious oppressed of Europe; but Penn was only anticipating the inevitable with the result that Pennsylvania leapfrogged over some of her less hospitable sister colonies, giving them by the example of her rapid growth a strong argument for greater toleration. And there was Rhode Island, which was a special case, an historical accident of sorts. But religious toleration could not become a fact of American life until the masters of those colonies with legally established religions allowed minority sects to practice their beliefs without effective penalty or hindrance. This came in the eighteenth century.

One component of growth that introduced a new factor making for a widening area of religious toleration was the non-English, non-Anglican immigration of the eighteenth century. After all, toleration hardly became a live question until raised by the presence in a colony of numerous dissenters to the locally established religion. German pietists and Scots-Irish Presbyterians poured mostly into burgeoning Pennsylvania where their religious beliefs were not at issue, but they also drifted in large numbers, particularly the Presbyterians, down into the backcountry of the Anglican South. There, far removed from the seats of power along the coast and with relatively few Anglicans among them, the backcountry Scots-Irish of Virginia, Carolina, and eventually Georgia simply practiced Presbyterianism with or without the sanction of colonial officials and despite occasional harassment from them. The preaching of George Whitefield and the ensuing Great Awakening in the South quickened the Presbyterian movement in the 1740s and 1750s and swept up still more thousands of colonists, nominal Anglicans or otherwise, into religious enthusiasm. The Methodist movement got under way within the Anglican church, and the Baptists began to make rapid headway particularly among the poor and religiously disaffected. In any event, immigration and conversion did its work during the middle decades of the eighteenth century. By the time of the Revolution, hardly one third of the whites in the South were members of the established church and probably as many more were something other than Anglican both in name and in fact.

It can be said that the introduction of such large numbers of adherents to dissenting faiths in effect presented the southern colonies with the inescapable fact of religious diversity, leaving them with no real option but to practice religious toleration. Yet it can be said with equal truth that this religious diversity was the product of the willingness of these colonies to accept dissenters and to deal with them in the spirit of England's Act of Toleration of 1689. The point in either case is that the established church found its position so undermined by the end of the colonial period that little was required to bring about disestablishment except to give legal ratification to something that already existed in fact. It remained, however, for the Revolution to bring to logical culmination the movement toward religious liberalization initiated by the immigration and Great Awakening of preceding decades. Before the end of the century the policy of religious toleration with the concomitant growth in the strength of religious dissent had borne its fruits in the South in the form of disestablishment of the Anglican church, separation of church and state, and religious liberty of sorts.

The growth of the colonies in the eighteenth century altered the religious situation in the South in ways other than by the introduction of Germans and the Scots-Irish Presbyterians. Perhaps almost as important were the effects of social change upon Anglicanism itself. It is fair to say that the established church contributed to its own undoing. How could it have been otherwise? In each colony the church had the sanction of provincial and imperial government as well as fixed support from public taxes. It numbered nearly all of the economic and social elite among its members, and they in turn held most of the important political offices, local and provincial, and dominated the colonial legislatures. The interesting thing is that the declining influence of Anglicanism after 1740 reflected not a deterioration but a steady strengthening in the position of the planter and merchant-planter aristocrat who sat in the halls of the legislature and in the pew of the parish church.

The arrangements this colonial elite had made to assure for themselves control over the church was one source of its weakness. Having early entrenched themselves in self-perpetuating parish vestries, the planters and their merchant allies used their control over the local churches to bring the clergy to heel and to prevent the development of a church hierarchy in the colonies. This made the vestrymen impregnable within the walls of their own individual churches, but Anglicanism was left seriously handicapped in meeting the challenge from the outside of widespread dissent. A less localized or decentralized church could far more readily have marshaled its combined resources to plant and succor new churches in the rapidly expanding territories of the colonies and so vie with dissenting churches for the souls of the brawling backcountrymen. It was in part this lack of Anglican activity on the frontier that the Reverend Thomas Bray had in mind when in 1701 he organized the Society for the Propagation of the Gospel in Foreign Parts, which provided the Anglican church in America with much of what missionary energy it generated in the eighteenth century.

More fundamental than any structural weakness, however, was the effect the increased wealth, self-assurance, and prestige of the southern planters and merchants had upon the established church and their attitude toward it. Secure for the moment in their position at the pinnacle of colonial society and enjoying to the full the pleasures and prerogatives this bestowed, the colonial elite in the South at midcentury felt less need than they once had for the solace of religion or for its organized support. Despite cases of individual piety, the rich and pleasure-loving gentlemen of Charleston were hardly religious enthusiasts even after Whitefield had cast his spell, and the tobacco planters of Virginia were often perfunctory at best in the performance of the rites of the church. The frequency with which Anglican vestries tolerated scandalously worldly and incompetent clergymen, or the absence of any clergymen at all, testified to this. Nor were these provincial sophisticates always immune to the appeal of facets of European Enlightenment thought which might raise doubts about revealed religion or about an Anglican monopoly of truth. If the practice of religious toleration in the face of growing dissent was three parts political prudence, it was at least one part religious indifference leavened with a dash of skepticism.

The Anglican church in the South not only let most of the backcountry go to the dissenters by default; it also left many commonfolk in the old parishes ripe for the picking by any who would promise them more vivid religious experiences and greater participation in church affairs. The Presbyterian's readiness to gather the harvest in eastern Virginia is a prime case in point. It all began in Hanover County just above the tidewater in the late 1730s when a bricklayer named Samuel Morris became dissatisfied with the preaching of his parish priest, the Reverend Patrick Henry, an uncle of his more famous namesake. Morris and several likeminded men began to meet regularly to read aloud the Epistles of St. Paul. In a few years Morris readers were numerous enough to require two meetinghouses in Hanover to hold them all. Summoned to Williamsburg in 1743 to explain themselves, the leaders of the dissident group learned for the first time, from Governor William Gooch himself, that their beliefs identified them as Presbyterians.

After returning home they got word that there was a Presbyterian minister on the other side of the Blue Ridge in the Valley of Virginia. The Valley had begun to fill up with Scots-Irish in the 1730s, and a Pennsylvania presbytery had sent William Robinson down to preach to a number of Christian societies the settlers had formed preparatory to constituting regular churches. Robinson came to Hanover before the end of the year and converted the two Morris meetinghouses into congregations of the Presbyterian Church. Itinerant ministers from one or another of the presbyteries in the middle colonies kept the Hanover churches going for several years despite growing opposition from Williamsburg. Not until after the arrival in 1748 of the gifted young Samuel Davies as permanent pastor did Presbyterianism become firmly established in eastern Virginia, however. Within two years Davies had secured licenses for seven Presbyterian meetinghouses in five counties in the piedmont. Five years later, the New York synod of the Presbyterian Church gave its recognition of the flourishing state of Virginia's Presbyterianism east of the mountains by constituting the Hanover presbytery.

As the account of the evolution of the Hanover presbytery suggests, the vigor of denominationalism in the middle colonies played a decisive role in the growth of dissent in the South. This is not to minimize the importance of Whitefield's preaching in arousing dissatisfaction with the state of the established church; but in order to capitalize on the religious ferment of the 1740s and 1750s southern Presbyterians, and in a different way even the Baptists, initially relied heavily on the support, guidance, and encouragement of their coreligionists in Pennsylvania, New Jersey, and New York. The religious revivalism which had begun in New Jersey in the 1720s with the preaching of Theodore J. Frelinghuysen of the Reformed Church and had been taken up by other ministers, most notably Presbyterians William and Gilbert Tennent of Pennsylvania, ushered in what has become known as the Great Awakening in the middle colonies. These revivalist preachers drew many of the unchurched to Christianity and quickened the religious pulse of many more with their fervent appeals to the emotions of ordinary people caught up in kaleidoscopic social change in eighteenth-century America. The Baptists were transformed into a dynamic church ready to do battle for the souls of a growing legion of susceptible farmers and artisans, and the Presbyterians emerged with a much broader base of support and with much greater organizational strength than before despite the resulting schism between the Old Sides and the New Sides.

What the Presbyterians, Baptists, and others were proving at midcentury was that a religious sect could sustain and extend itself in America without either the sanction or the financial support of the state. Even as they were demonstrating the viability of independent denominations, they were also preparing Americans for acceptance of what few could yet fully accept: that a people could countenance in its midst a multiplicity of churches varying in doctrine and form without giving offense to God's truth or endangering His cause. Full acceptance of this would bear the implication that religious sects were not rivals but fellow workers in the same vineyard and that none laid claim to be the exclusive bearer of the Truth. Even if one grants the importance of the rationalist thought of men like Jefferson and Madison, it is difficult to see how the Revolutionary generation in the South could have embraced separation of church and state or been willing to experiment with religious liberty had the middle colonies not earlier shown the way.

Congregationalist New England like the Anglican South felt the shock waves of religious revivalism emanating from the preaching of Whitefield and men like Frelinghuysen and the Tennents in the middle colonies. And then in the 1740s the New England church was shaken to its Puritan roots by one of its own, the mighty Jonathan Edwards, who is generally deemed the finest theologian of eighteenth-century America. The established church, however, emerged from the Great Awakening stronger than it had been since the days of the Puritan commonwealth of Massachusetts-Bay. Edwards and his followers brought about a rejuvenation of Congregationalism, which was in part a recovery of some of the Calvinist thrust of seventeenth-century Puritanism and in part an adaptation of Puritan beliefs and traditions to the altered circumstances of mid-eighteenth-century New England.

The established church in New England was in a much better position to ride out the storm stirred up by the Great Awakening than was the established church in the South. The hold of Congregationalism on the generality of people in the New England towns had remained relatively strong during the expansive first decades of the eighteenth century, and the new immigrants, German pietist and Scotch Presbyterian, had largely passed New England by for the fertile lands of Pennsylvania and the southern colonies. Yet the Great Awakening did sharpen the voices of dissent to the church established by the Standing Order of New England, particularly the voices of the Baptists. Anglicans, Quakers, and Anabaptists had long been tolerated within the colonies of the Congregational establishment, even to the point of being exempted from the payment of taxes to support the New England church; but at midcentury the Baptists, fast growing in numbers and fervor, rejected mere toleration and pushed for disestablishment. An entrenched and revitalized Congregationalism was able to withstand and then beat back the challenge of the Baptists, and not even the force of Revolutionary ideology and change could dislodge the church from its favored legal position.

As both purveyor and product of the Great Awakening, denominationalism was its prime beneficiary. The leading denominations with new self-assertiveness and heightened self-awareness moved on several fronts to maintain their momentum and to consolidate their gains. As important in the long run as their proselytizing or missionary activities and their agitation against church establishments were the measures they adopted to provide educational opportunities—and religious indoctrination—for their communicants and training for their clergy. Between 1746 and 1769, the Presbyterian, Baptist, Dutch Reformed, Anglican, and Congregational churches each utilized some of the growing wealth of its membership to found a college. These new colleges—Princeton, Brown, Rutgers, Columbia, and Dartmouth—like their three predecessors, Harvard, William and Mary, and Yale, were called into existence to turn out ministers to fill the pulpits in the churches of the various denominations. Here in the decades immediately preceding the Revolution, sectarianism placed its imprint firmly and lastingly on higher education in America.

Important though it was that religious denominations rather than any other agency in colonial society assumed the function of providing higher education for Americans, more important still are certain approaches to education and educational institutions which the sectarian connection laid down and confirmed. As the instrument of fractionalized Protestantism in the colonies, for instance, American higher education from the start was itself fractionalized, decentralized, dispersed. Counting the nonsectarian College of Philadelphia begun in 1754, there were in 1769 nine colleges in colonial America strung out from Virginia to New Hampshire, a far cry from the clustered colleges of Oxford and Cambridge. However ill suited to advancing the cause of pure scholarship, the colonists' approach to higher education which permitted the creation of institutions almost at random and at will proved ideal for the purposes of America as it became a great federal empire stretching from the Atlantic to the Pacific and a great democratic republic bent upon exposing more and more of its youth to the joys of college life.

The religious denominations that gave birth to colleges in the colonial period and to many more like them during the first century of the Republic retained control over their institutions and shaped them to their sectarian purposes. Outside support and control of educational institutions, which represented a sharp break with European practice, became the set pattern for American education, higher or lower. Lacking a medieval patrimony or access to accumulated wealth, and created on one fine day out of whole cloth, the colonial school or college had to rely for its support upon the agency that brought it into being, whether an individual, a religious sect, or the public. Control of the purse strings permitted colonial sectarians to call the tune for church schools and colleges, and allowed freeholders to do the same for the schools maintained by the New England towns. Outside control of educational institutions became so firmly fixed in the eighteenth century that when the state ultimately assumed as one of its major responsibilities the education of its citizenry, the political supervision of public schools and colleges was taken as a matter of course. The government of educational institutions by agencies made up of men not otherwise connected with them has exposed American education to peculiar dangers and imposed upon it unfamiliar burdens; but it also has made education, public and private, acutely responsive to the aspirations and needs of American society, and education has received in return an extraordinary measure of public support.

The rapid evolution of colonial society prompted by material growth in the first half of the eighteenth century affected education in ways perhaps more fundamental, if less tangible, than giving rise to the expansion of sectarian schooling. The mobility and uprootedness of colonial life and the opportunities it afforded for self-advancement gradually produced profound changes in educational attitudes. Although these altered views about the forms and functions of education suitable for the new American society did not really receive overt expression until the Revolutionary era, the New England Puritans early concluded that they could not rely solely on the traditional molders of the child's mind and conduct —the family, community, and the church. Not even these indispensables could be taken for granted in the first stages of settlement on a frontier.

The further dispersal and differentiation of the colonists in the eighteenth century resulting from an accelerated movement of settlers into the interior, the introduction into the population of disparate elements from Ireland and Germany, and the emergence of a well-defined social and economic elite underscored the fallacy of assuming that parental, communal, and pastoral guidance would automatically suffice to preserve and transmit cherished religious and cultural values in the New World. A dawning realization that education of the young was not a ready by-product of living in society if that society itself was at best in the act of forming opened the way for viewing the educational process in childhood as something that could be deliberately planned, separately organized, and used by society for its own purposes.

The point is not that the colonists were first to discover formal education for the young or its utility but that the American condition led them to seize upon it as a weapon to hold at bay the forces of encroaching barbarism. In the seventeenth century this was seen as foiling the "ould deluder Satan" and after 1776 as instilling public virtue essential to the health of the thirteen new republics; but the schools established by public law in the New England towns and by religious sects in the middle colonies as well as the multiplying sectarian colleges were all evidence of a conscious effort to shore up the rising scaffolding of American civilization—and of an awareness that formal education was suitable for this purpose. Formalized education was becoming in the eighteenth century central to the American experiment.

The unprecedented opportunities for personal advancement that American life afforded eventually led to the development of a system of education designed to make available to the ordinary man whatever learning he required to take advantage of the opportunities open to him. Although this was hardly even a distant ideal in colonial times, the logic of the colonial situation was making for just such an eventuality. No models handed down by the Old World would for long answer the purposes of the highly fluid and mobile society of eighteenth-century America. With remarkable prescience Benjamin Franklin called for schooling that would fit youth for "any business, calling, or profession" and took a step toward this goal with evening schools for his junta of printers, scriveners, shoemakers, and joiners. Franklin's own rise from printer's devil to world figure revealed how far divorced ultimately from social reality in America was any system of education which sought to train men for predetermined stations in life. Although the colonials left it to the future to broaden educational curricula and to proliferate educational institutions to meet the requirements of an expanding society, these came more easily because of what eighteenth-century Americans had done. The colonists bequeathed a tradition of creating educational institutions for specific social purposes and of vesting control of these institutions in outsiders who could be trusted not to lose sight of the functions an institution was supposed to perform. What remained was for the public to see the need and accept the cost of providing such institutions for the education of all.

It can be argued with considerable justice that securing a degree of education more than anything else opened the way for a man's rise to a position of leadership in his community in eighteenth-century America, particularly on the frontier. For instance, when upcountrymen made a successful bid for a share of political power in frontier Georgia in the 1780s, the only discernible common characteristic that set the leaders selected by the upcountrymen apart from their constituency was their superior educational attainments. Such a high premium was put on education partly because even its rudiments remained beyond the reach of many, perhaps most, Americans. Opportunities for schooling grew progressively rarer for most people the farther south from New England they lived and the farther inland from the coast. The rate of illiteracy in colonial America was always high, how high is not certain; but the literate segment of the population was large enough to provide leadership in all aspects and at all levels of life. And they set its tone in a way that reflected America's European origins and its continued dependence on European forms and ideas even as the stage was being set for political separation.

When young George Washington headed out in 1753 for the Ohio country and, as it happened, set in motion the chain of events that led to the denouement of 1776, thousands of ignorant blacks were toiling on the plantations and still more thousands of unschooled whites, farmers and artisans, townsfolk and frontiersmen, were tilling their fields or peddling their wares and services. Then there were the others, men of the better sort as they viewed themselves. These were the colonists who scanned the pages of their weekly or biweekly gazettes and thereby learned more of the doings of the courts of Europe than of their fellow provincials in neighboring colonies; who bought, and sometimes read, books and pamphlets from London giving the latest word on law, the science of politics, theology, history, natural science, architecture, horticulture, animal husbandry, or manners; who built sound houses in the countryside or, increasingly, in towns like Boston and Salem, Providence, Newport, New Haven, New York, Perth Amboy, Philadelphia, Annapolis, Williamsburg, New Bern, Charleston, and Savannah, and furnished them well or less well with English plate, china, and furniture; who might or might not have a carriage or ever take a voyage to London but almost always kept at least one servant and sired children with seeming gusto and certain fecundity; who supported schools or hired tutors for their children and if they could manage sent their sons to the local college or better still to the universities of England and Scotland; who supervised the churches, managed the courts from bench and bar, led the militia, governed town and county, sat in the legislature, filled the governor's council and the administrative offices of the colony, and generally coped with the lesser sort below and with king and governor above; who raised crops for sale, practiced law and medicine, preached and taught and traded; who, in short, were making America what they wanted it to be, making it their own.

Chapter VIII

The Seeds of Disunion

Colonists with at least a bit of education and some means wrote the American story as it unfolded in the first half of the eighteenth century. It was they who to a considerable degree not only engineered the explosive growth of the colonies but also controlled and adapted the institutions that permitted colonial society to cope with its own rapid expansion. A sequential narrative of political management by this colonial elite has often served as the history of one colony or another for the five or six decades before the Revolutionary movement got under way. Whatever the limitations of this approach, it is certainly true that one can hardly hope to gain any real understanding of eighteenth-century America, or of its Revolution, unless he has some knowledge of the process by which representative assemblies came to occupy a pivotal position in colonial government.

Colonials on the make always looked for political leadership to the planters and merchants who had already made it, and to their lawyer allies; but after 1700 the numbers both of those soon to take their place among the colony's elite and of those counting themselves already members of that elite grew markedly from decade to decade. Furthermore, this pool of emergent and emerging leaders formed only the most conspicuous part of a hustling, bustling society of parvenus keenly aware they were onto a good thing and always on the lookout for ways to protect and promote what they had going for them. How this politically active segment of the colonial population, which for that age was remarkably large (much larger than was once thought), came to terms with internal expansion and with external supervision from Britain is the story of the evolving of political institutions and the fixing of political assumptions and practices. It is also the story of the forming of the political matrix out of which the generation of politicians who were to build a new nation emerged.

Viewed in general terms, what we have here is the process by which a new elite gained political authority commensurate with its advancing economic and social position in the community. The chief vehicle by which these colonials translated economic success and social standing into political influence was membership in the lower house of the provincial legislature, to which their neighbors elected them. Men of property had been choosing delegates to colonial assemblies, and serving as delegates themselves, almost from the beginning of English colonization in America. Late in the seventeenth century King William III effectively confirmed the representative principle as a fixed element of the colonial constitution. The recent debacle brought on by Edmund Andros' attempt in the late 1680s to govern the Dominion of New England without a representative assembly had revealed that it continued to be as necessary for the colonists to participate in their own government as it had been when the burgesses were first called to Jamestown in 1619 or when the assistants first sat in the general court of Massachusetts in the 1630s. To hold the allegiance and command the obedience of a colonial people in the absence of overwhelming force has never been easy.

By acquiescing in the general practice of having an elective assembly act as one branch of the colonial legislature, the English had tacitly conceded that no colonial legislature could enact a law or levy a tax without the consent of the representatives of the colony's electorate; but that was all they had conceded, or ever would. The king's government in London, and his officials in America, were to set public policy and see to it that their rightful orders and instructions were carried out. It was the colonists' duty to obey.

Until well into the eighteenth century the assemblies in Virginia and other royal colonies, though sometimes contentious and even defiant, usually functioned much as royal officials believed a lower house of a colonial legislature should: they continued to approve or reject what the governor and the council proposed and seldom took the initiative in legislation. This was to change, however. In the expansive third and fourth decades of the eighteenth century, colonial entrepreneurs on the rise found their private interests increasingly affected by decisions being made in the statehouse. Political decisions affecting such things as currency, land, prices, taxes, credit, appropriations, servants, and slaves were nearly always of considerable concern to large-scale merchants or planters in a colony. Being prudent men, they as the main beneficiaries of the American bonanza either went themselves or sent each other to the legislature in each colony to protect and advance their personal interests. They no longer hesitated to initiate measures favorable to their own interest and to oppose those contrary to it. And because they did so with considerable success, they often found themselves at odds with the governor and his council. The first duty of the governor, particularly if he were a royal governor, was to uphold the interests of Britain within the colony. The dictum that whatever was good for the mother country would surely benefit her colonies seldom persuaded colonial leaders to sacrifice without protest their own immediate advantage to that of Britain. It is therefore not surprising that political life in the colonies was punctuated by the periodic eruption of controversy between the governor and the lower house of the legislature.

Only rarely did men of affairs in England or America perceive in these random, recurring hassles over immediate and limited issues anything more than superfluous confirmation of colonial obstreperousness or of the intransigence of royal officials. Yet historians have since come to view them as vital links in a chain that by 1765 had radically altered political life in British America. The representative assemblies did not win every battle, but they won most of them. The cumulative effect of this, and of other things, was the gradual, fitful, but seemingly inexorable extension of the power of the assembly in colony after colony. What the assembly gained the governor and council ordinarily lost, since the lower house could widen its sphere of authority within the established government of the colony only by encroaching upon the sphere of legislative and executive authority enjoyed by the governor and his council. The powers of government were not being notably enlarged; they were being redistributed. In 1765 when the Stamp Act finally brought the colonial assemblies into direct conflict with the Parliament of Great Britain, it became apparent that the powers of the governor and council had slipped away so considerably that the two were no match for an aroused assembly.

In the process by which political initiative in the legislatures passed from officials appointed by the king or proprietors into the hands of locally elected representatives, one might say that each assembly reached the critical point in its rise when the governor and council in the colony went more or less permanently on the defensive. In most colonies this had happened by the 1740s and in some well before that time. Colonial participation in Britain's long war beginning in America in 1754 against the French and Indians gave every colonial legislature wider scope for political maneuver; and by the time peace came in 1763 most of the assemblies had established something very like dominance in colonial government. During the 1730s Governor William Gooch of Virginia had taken pains to get along with the burgesses; for his successors a few decades later it had become less a matter of getting along with the people's representatives than of going along with them.

This shift in power from one element of provincial government to another was largely the product of a long succession of minor changes in the way politicians conducted the business of government. As lawyers have always known, in law and politics how a thing is done often proves more important than what is done. While firmly attached to the old procedures by which they guarded the independence of the lower house of the colonial legislature and exercised its traditional authority, the representatives were always ready to adopt any new procedure that promised to give the assembly greater autonomy or greater influence. At issue in one way or another in nearly every important dispute between the lower house and the governor or council before 1760 was the proper way to proceed in managing some aspect of public affairs. Proper procedure might be overtly at issue as when the South Carolina house of assembly informed the council that it would no longer countenance the council's amending money bills, or when it sought to deny the council the right to participate in auditing public accounts.

More often the assembly, and sometimes the governor or council, challenged established procedures by provoking a fight over the payment of a particular official's salary or a specific public account. These were in reality contests to determine how an official should be appointed, how public moneys should be appropriated or disbursed, or how an account should be audited. Usually the representatives were the ones seeking to change the mode of appointment or payment, and always in a way to give the lower house an enlarged role. If the house succeeded in its efforts to pay, or not to pay, an official or an account, the next time round it would pay or not pay in the same way, often without provoking a fuss. In this way, the lines were gradually redrawn between the authority of the colonial assemblies and the prerogatives of the governors and their councils.

Early or late, sometimes with a struggle and sometimes without, each colonial house of assembly secured its flank by establishing extensive control over its own composition and proceedings. And it learned how to use its tax power as a wedge for penetrating into nearly every aspect of public finance, dislodging or hemming in the governor and council at each step. The process varied from colony to colony and the result was never precisely the same; but by 1763 the lower house of the assembly was the prime political force in twelve of the thirteen colonies, whether royal, chartered, or proprietary. And the lower house in the thirteenth colony, Georgia, would shortly come into its own.

The British House of Commons always served as the model for these representative assemblies as they were making their bids for an enlarged role in colonial politics. The broad financial powers of the House of Commons served as both inspiration and justification for many of the assembly's pretensions to powers and functions vested in the provincial governor and council by the king, and in the end the colonists succeeded in converting their assemblies into something very like petty Houses of Commons.

Had the developments of the first half of the eighteenth century in America not culminated in revolution, which is certainly conceivable, the emergence of these representative bodies would appear to us now as it did then, in about 1750. We would be studying the rise of the colonial assemblies simply to discover how a dependent people managed to gain wide control over their political affairs while remaining within the confines of an imperial structure. And this would reveal something we still should not overlook, that the true genius of the old British Empire was its unwitting capacity for allowing political institutions to adapt themselves to the realities of social and economic change. Unfortunately, it was precisely this capacity that the rulers of the empire lost for a time after 1763. Thanks in part to this lapse, the Revolution did occur, casting a different light on past politics in the colonies and placing the emergence of powerful representative assemblies in a quite different perspective.

What happened to these assemblies between 1700 and 1763 provides one of the best clues as to why it was and how it was that the colonies were able to revolt against British rule in 1776. Yet the movement toward independence was not simply a continuation of the "rise of the Assembly." Partial self-government did not lead directly, as if by a law of nature, to a demand for total independence. Rather, it was the fear of the loss of self-government and the consequent loss of personal liberty that pushed the Americans to the point of revolt. Only by appreciating what the colonists and their assemblies had won and stood to lose can one make sense out of the colonial reaction to British policy after 1763. But it was not only the role the representative assemblies had come to play in colonial life and politics that gave the colonists a vital stake in opposing the new and extensive intrusion of British power into the colonies after the French and Indian War. The well-established popular assembly also provided a base of operations from which the colonists could make their opposition felt. Over the years the representative assemblies had taught the colonists the value of political action, had trained them to think and act in political terms. Consequently, by 1763 there were in every colony men experienced in political tactics and accustomed to responding politically to any challenge to their position. It was they who succeeded during the next decade in organizing and leading in America the opposition to parliamentary measures. Subsequently they also proved able to conduct a successful revolution, the rarest thing in politics. The colonists' quest for power through their representative assemblies nurtured an aggregation of highly developed political animals, the likes of whom few societies have produced.

The shift of power in each colonial legislature from the executive branch to the lower house had ramifications extending far beyond the bounds of the individual colonies. This transformation of the colonial constitution (that is, form of government) in the first half of the eighteenth century altered the constitutional make-up of the empire as a whole. Virginia and Massachusetts, New York and South Carolina, were after all component parts of the empire, subordinate to the king in Parliament across the sea. The colonial executive officers were the instruments upon which the British government relied to preserve the due subordination of Britain's colonies. Any loss in the authority of these officials and gain in that of the colonists' assemblies represented a comparable decline in Britain's own effective authority.

High officials in Britain, particularly the King-in-Council, the secretary of state for the southern department, and the Board of Trade, time and again rejected concessions that the colonial assemblies had wrested from provincial governors; but whether through oversight or through indifference, or out of political expediency, they also often acquiesced in practices that clearly contravened the king's instructions to his provincial governors. The failure of officials in London to check the lower house of the colonial legislature in its drive to tame the upper house and to usurp many of the powers of the executive was not in itself fatal to good order and workable relationships in the empire. What did prove fatal in the end was their refusal, or inability, to come to terms with the consequences of their laxity. As Britain's disastrous American policy in the 1760s demonstrates, the managers of the empire did not let the fact that the structure of colonial politics and of imperial relationships had plainly been decisively altered affect their long-held view of the role a colonial assembly should properly play or the prerogatives a provincial governor should rightfully enjoy.

It is fair to say that Britain's notion of what a colony should be, of what rights and powers its inhabitants should be allowed and what prerogatives the governor should retain, was fixed in the late seventeenth century and remained essentially unchanged until the end. With every passing year in the eighteenth century what the colonies in fact were becoming was less and less what the British thought they were, or ought to be. The king's instructions issued to Governor Spotswood in 1710 were a fairly accurate description of how Virginia's government worked in 1710; the almost identical instructions given Governor Fauquier in 1758 bore little resemblance to how Virginia's government was actually functioning by midcentury. When in a political system the disparity between theory and practice becomes as great as it had become in the British Empire at the time George Grenville took office as the king's chief minister in 1763, the danger is that the pressure of events will push men in power to act as if theory were fact, or to undertake to make it so. One of the driving forces behind the colonial policy that Grenville inaugurated at the end of the French and Indian War, and that his successors pursued in one way or another until they drove Britain's colonies into rebellion, was the determination "to return the affairs of the colonies to their proper channel." If by this was meant forcing the colonies back into seventeenth-century molds, it was clearly too late for that.

Whatever the options remaining open to the British and the Americans to alter the direction of events in the decade before 1776, the events set in motion by decisions made in London after the war with France in 1763 did lead directly to the declaration of independence. The French and Indian War (1754-1763), which in 1756 spread to Europe where it is called the Seven Years' War, therefore marked the climax, in some ways even the final chapter, of colonial development along the Atlantic seaboard of British North America. The few years remaining after the war before the breakup of the old empire in 1776 were marked by turmoil and conflict. Until 1763 the English colonies were in the process of maturing *as colonies,* and their history is the history of colonial development; in the decade after 1763 the thirteen colonies were being transformed into states ready for independence, and their story belongs to the history of the Revolution.

As one would expect, the war with France and its outcome had a great deal to do with this abrupt change in direction. The war itself enabled the representative assemblies in America to improve and solidify their position in colonial government. It also gave British officialdom some inkling of just how far things had gone in America. This, and the far-reaching consequences of the war and of British victory, put enormous pressure on the imperial government to do something about the colonies before they got completely out of hand. Britain's critical need for men and money to carry on the fight against the French and their Indian allies in North America had given the lower houses of the colonial legislatures the opportunity to flex their muscles. It was they who had decided how money should be raised, and how much, for troops and supplies in aid of the mother country. The mixed responses to the British when they instructed the colonial legislatures to provide funds to prosecute the war brought home to the king's officials as never before just how little they could rely upon the ability of appointed officials in colonial government to carry out imperial policy. The British government also had learned that not only was it unable to command the colonists' obedience, neither could it count upon their voluntary cooperation. Rarely did a colonial legislature provide all that was requested in the way of troops or supplies, and individual colonists had persisted in trading with the enemy in defiance both of the ancient Navigation Acts and of common decency. It is little wonder that the British had started to make moves to tighten up the administration of the empire well before the fighting was over.

Armed conflict between Britain and France in North America had begun, or had been resumed, when the French ambushed Major George Washington's detachment of Virginia militia at Great Meadows in the wilds of Pennsylvania in the late spring of 1754. The war that ensued, sometimes called the Great War for Empire as well as the French and Indian War, was at the time only the greatest in a series of wars between Britain and France dating back to the seventeenth century, each fought on the continent of Europe and in North America, and on the high seas. In the first of these wars, King William's War or the War of the League of Augsburg (1689-1697), the English battled to block Louis XIV's drive to establish French hegemony on the continent. As an island power lying off the coast of Europe, England could not afford to sit idly by while a single power by conquest or alliance united all of Europe. If France should ever become so far master of Europe as to be free of any threat from her neighbors and at the same time have access to the combined human and material resources of most of the continent, Great Britain would be in grave danger. Through-

out the eighteenth century, the British sought allies on the continent and subsidized them to contain France. They also went to war
twice more in the first half of the century: Queen Anne's War
(1702-1713), or the War of the Spanish Succession, and King
George's War (1739/40-1748), or the War of the Austrian Succession. Britain's victory in 1763 did not, of course, mark the end of
the Anglo-French rivalry: still to come were the war for American
independence and after 1789 the wars of the French Revolution
and Napoleon. After the final overthrow of Napoleon in 1815, the
British, protected by the English Channel, at last true mistress of the
seas, and made rich and powerful by a great industrial machine and
world empire, had little to fear from a divided Europe until the rise
of modern Germany in the twentieth century. It was not until the
destruction of Nazi Germany in World War II, and the emergence
of the United States and the Soviet Union as new kinds of world
powers, however, that the basic tenets of Britain's foreign policy
forged in the eighteenth century suddenly became largely irrele-
vant.

North America loomed large in Britain's calculations and moves
in her bitter rivalry with France in the eighteenth century, as did
the United States in Britain's struggles with Germany in the twentieth. But in a far different way. By the time William of Orange
came to the English throne in 1689 and threw the weight of England against the triumphant forces of France's Louis XIV, France
and England, as well as Spain, had established empires in continental North America. The French had first settled on the St. Lawrence
River in 1608, the year after the English came to Jamestown; by the
second half of the seventeenth century, eastern Canada was theirs.
Under the leadership of the vigorous Comte de Frontenac they
then extended French control through trade and alliances with the
Indians up the St. Lawrence into the Great Lakes region, along the
Ohio, and down the Mississippi. Both trade and friendship with the
Indians were buttressed by military outposts and Christian missions.
There were French farmers in Quebec, of course; but unlike the
English colonists most of the French who came to America in the
early years did not settle in compact and contiguous farming com-
munities. Instead, they traveled the great rivers to trade with the
Indians, particularly for furs to supply the European market. The

French empire in Canada and west of the Alleghenies and the English colonies along the Atlantic seaboard were in many ways studies in contrast when the Old World rivalries and ambitions of their mother countries first drew them into conflict.

In King William's War and in the two subsequent Anglo-French wars, neither the French nor the English establishment in America was in real danger of being wiped out or taken over by the other. Nor was this the aim of either of the rival powers. Upon the outbreak of war in Europe, the French forces in America or their Indian allies would resume their raids on outlying settlements in New England and New York, and less often in the South. The English colonists, for their part, were likely to organize expeditions into French territory, their favorite target being the fortress at Louisburg which guarded the entrance to the St. Lawrence. At the end of each war, the British were ready to trade off Louisburg or whatever French territory her Anglo-American forces might have won for French concessions in Europe. This often meant simply a return to the *status quo ante bellum.* Like it or not, the English colonists fought in America to maintain the balance of power in Europe.

Warfare in America during the half century after 1689 undoubtedly had its impact on the psyche of colonial society; it also must have affected the rate and pattern of economic growth, of population movement, of land settlement and utilization, of the importation of slaves, of trading activity, of the expansion and contraction of the money supply, and of the boom-and-bust cycle that was already a familiar phenomenon. Yet the precise nature of the effect of the wars on these things remains largely a mystery. Historians who seem never to tire of tracing out the ramifying consequences of every subsequent American war have generally been content to describe the scalpings, count the casualties, and list the peace terms of the three Anglo-French wars fought in America between 1689 and 1748.

The French and Indian War on every count is another matter, however. The war itself did not follow the usual pattern, its outcome was quite different, and its consequences have been thoroughly explored and carefully documented. After William Pitt took over the direction of the war in 1757, British regulars and colonial militiamen in America overcame earlier reverses and in the next three years captured most of the important French strong points in Canada, including Quebec city itself, and in the Ohio country. British forces met with similar success in India and the Caribbean, and on the high seas. Meanwhile, in Europe, Frederick the Great of Prussia fought back from the brink of disaster and with his allies defeated the French army. France was left with no hostage in Europe to use as a pawn at the peace table to regain her lost holdings abroad. In the Treaty of Paris of 1763, France gave up its empire on the North American continent, ceding to Britain its claims to Canada and to the land lying to the west of Britain's seaboard colonies, as well as Spanish Florida. All of a sudden, Britain's American empire was vastly expanded in size and French power was removed from the continent. This clear-cut victory proved to be a mixed blessing.

The problems facing the rulers of the British Empire were now great and complex. Enormous reaches of lands, thinly peopled by hostile Indians and alien Frenchmen, had to be brought under control, administered, and defended. The prospects of hordes of land-hungry settlers and speculators swarming from the old colonies through the mountain passes into the Ohio and Mississippi country raised the specter of constant conflict and virtual chaos in the transmontane West, increasing the urgency for the British government to act promptly and decisively. Its difficulties in dealing with the newly acquired territory were compounded by the degree to which each individual colony had in the past conducted its own relations with the Indians on its borders, working out trade agreements and securing cessions of land for white settlers. Mere general supervision of colonial initiative in Indian affairs would hardly do in the changed circumstances.

Whatever else the British should or should not do to incorporate the French territories into her American empire, there could be no doubt at Whitehall about the necessity of stationing British regulars in the West. A show of force was clearly needed to keep the peace. To maintain a standing army in America, however, would cost money, a great deal of money. This in turn would place a heavy strain on the British Treasury at a time it was already seriously overburdened. The recent war with France had been the most expensive by far in Britain's history. The public debt of £100 million was so unprecedentedly high as to be frightening. Annual payments of the interest on the national debt alone would exceed normal public expenditures in past years of peace. Any chance of reducing wartime tax rates, particularly high on land, would be sharply diminished by outlays for stationing British regulars in America.

The realization borne in upon British officials during the recent war that the colonies in America were certainly not fulfilling all the functions of colonies or always acting as proper colonies should prompted the consideration of what might be done to make them more useful and profitable to the hard-pressed mother country. In particular, there was the galling awareness that smuggling by colonial merchants had for many years robbed Britain of what was perhaps a large part of her lawful profits from colonial trade. Pitt had tightened up the enforcement of the acts of trade during the war, but further steps had to be taken to maintain and improve the machinery for regulating colonial commerce. Britain could hardly be expected to bear the burden of supporting and defending the colonies unless they served their proper purpose, not to say sole purpose, which was to create profits for Britain herself from their trade. Britain's victory over France and the terms of the treaty of peace had demonstrated beyond question the great value of the imperial connection to the colonies in America. After all, they were the main beneficiaries of the expulsion of France from American shores. It was only fair that they should be made to accord to Britain what they themselves conceded was rightfully hers—a monopoly of their foreign trade.

Undoubtedly behind these calculations about the need for more customs officers and ships to enforce trade regulations and for troops to pacify the resentful French and Indians in the West lay thoughts of checking the colonies' alarming drift toward "independency." But this was moving onto dangerous terrain. The less one said about it, perhaps the better.

At an earlier or later day, the British government might have been content not to go much beyond its undoubted right to control the trade of the colonies in its attempt both to impose greater discipline on the colonists and to secure a greater return on its

American investment. And it might have succeeded in achieving its legitimate objectives had it vigorously and persistently asserted its authority along traditional and accepted lines, such as the regulation of trade. Any colonial resistance would then have been robbed of most of the legitimacy it did have in the 1760s, and the growth of colonial autonomy would have been at least slowed if not checked.

But to adopt a consistent and restrained imperial policy and to carry it through despite domestic pressures was quite beyond the British government as it was constituted in the 1760s. One complicating factor was that, after 1763, the House of Commons for the first time in more than half a century became very much involved in setting colonial policy. The Commons were inevitably drawn in because of the pressing need for public funds to support the civil and military establishments in the enlarged empire. As a composite —or the embodiment—of local and private interests in the British Isles, the House of Commons was not likely to take the long view of imperial matters unless led to it by men of superior vision. Such leadership was not forthcoming. It hardly could have been. The government of Great Britain at this juncture was simply not suited to meet the demands being put upon it as the monitor of a far-flung empire. It was at a stage in which for a time no man or group of men, no matter how wise and forceful, could establish a reliable political base from which to control events.

After coming to the throne in 1760, the young George III wasted little time in getting rid of the men who had managed colonial affairs for his predecessor. Old hands like the Duke of Newcastle had appreciated the wisdom of letting sleeping dogs lie when dealing with the colonial assemblies; but the new breed of ministers beginning with George Grenville in 1763 were not of a mind to play so passive a role even if changed circumstances had not made the old policy of salutary neglect no longer feasible. What made matters worse was how extraordinarily difficult it was for the ministers to exercise effective leadership of any sort. The ministry was composed of the men in Parliament who held the great public offices and with the King were supposed to formulate public policy and see to its execution. The ministers gained and held office at the pleasure of the King, but they could function together as an effective government only if they could collectively command the support of a majority of the members of the House of Commons. That is, they had to have votes as well as the offices if they were to keep the government going. Given the temperament and inexperience of the new King and the nature of the unreformed House of Commons in 1760, the chances of any ministry pleasing both King and Commons was remote. And the chances of any such ministry's dealing in a boldly constructive way with the harsh realities of social unrest at home and political dissension in the colonies was even more remote.

By the time Britain signed a peace treaty with France in Paris in 1763, it was clear just how remote both these things were. The young King had almost immediately begun his search for a ministry to his liking which could manage the House of Commons. He did not find it, nor was he to find it anytime soon. The resignation as first minister of George's personal favorite, Lord Bute, in 1762 set in motion what was to be a decade of political instability in the upper reaches of the British government. As long as the political equation remained what it was at the outset of George's reign, there would be shifting factional alliances in Parliament, a rapid turnover of ministries, and the concentration of political energies upon gaining and holding office to the exclusion of nearly everything else.

Given what the colonists had become by 1763, and now having been freed of dependence upon British arms by the expulsion of France from the continent, they would have posed a problem for even the wisest ministry. Like men in most societies, the backwoods farmers in America, which is what most of the colonists were, were a mixed lot, but it is fair to say that on the whole they were more self-assertive and self-reliant, more hopeful, more versatile, politically more active and experienced than were the peasants of Europe. Or so it has been said, and so it would seem. These are qualities men developed in order to survive in the seventeenth century and to get ahead in the eighteenth. Pretty clearly, too, survival followed by personal advancement beyond anything once dreamed of transformed into something like conviction what for most peoples remains only a prayerful hope: that God had singled out Americans for His particular care. The sense of being under

God's special protection may not have been as immediate or universal in 1760 as it had been in Massachusetts in the 1630s; but the assumption can be seen lurking in many a private communication and public pronouncement of eighteenth-century Americans. As was brought out during the Revolution, hardworking farmers in Massachusetts and Virginia along the way also came to harbor the illusion that they and their neighbors were somehow more worthy of God's care, more virtuous, than either the downtrodden poor or the profligate rich of the Old World. An uncertain mix was brewing in America. Men like this—men of personal competence with a sense of their own worth who are confident of God's special favor and of the general superiority of their society—do not make the most manageable subjects for a king ruling from afar.

The more successful among these colonials in eighteenth-century America, the ones who became the leaders of colonial society, were far more like and far less removed from the generality of their fellow inhabitants than were members of the ruling classes in Europe. Here lies much of the explanation for why politics took some of the turns it did in eighteenth-century America. The leaders and the led felt many of the same stimuli and usually reacted to them in the same ways. Deference to one's social superiors on the one hand and conflict between economic and social groups on the other were both ingredients of colonial politics, but so were a relative lack of distinction between high and low and a relative lack of conflict between rich and poor characteristic of politics in the American colonies. Long before opposition to British measures and the heavy-handed tactics of the patriots had forged a revolutionary consensus of sorts, a rough similarity of outlook and circumstance in a broad spectrum of colonial society had been the basis of a working political consensus among the inhabitants of most of the colonies. Had this not been so, republicanism could hardly have taken root so quickly in 1776, and political democracy would have been delayed longer than it was.

The colonial leaders at midcentury lacked neither self-confidence nor a sense of their own importance. Many set themselves up as men of learning familiar with the ways of the outside world. Yet even most of these, whatever their pretensions, as late as 1760 remained at bottom touchy provincials. A haughty British official in Boston or Savannah could reduce a local merchant or planter to helpless rage, and chance encounters on a visit home to England could raise the hackles of even the most loyal and admiring colonial. Many of them suffered as well all the uncertainties and insecurities that plague the newly rich and the newly arrived. A young colonial seeking his fortune might be buoyed by an awareness of how fast and how far an enterprising man might rise in America. Having made his fortune, however, he could not forget how quickly and how low a little bad luck or bad judgment could reduce him.

Unlike the complacent English squire who could look back upon a long line of country gentlemen preceding him and could confidently assume he was siring an even longer line to follow, the edgy colonial at the top of his little heap could take nothing for granted. What it required in acumen, close application, and long experience to become a great colonial merchant or planter—and it took a great deal of each plus more than a little bit of luck—bred in some the kind of self-assurance that put them at ease with themselves and the world, but it also made most of the colonial grandees aware how dependent they were and ever would be upon the freedom to manage their own affairs—within the familiar if sometimes irksome limits set by their colonial status. By midcentury certainly, colonial merchants and planters were finding in their control of the local assembly and the leverage it had acquired in colonial government their greatest assurance that they would not suddenly be put at a disadvantage by capricious changes in the rules of the game. Self-assured and self-doubting; optimistic and fearful; men of acknowledged position and importance at home but unknown and little accounted outside their parish, county, or town, except perhaps in the provincial capital; masters of many acres and slaves but deep in debt; traders whose fortunes were forever riding on the outcome of a distant voyage where a break in the market, the insolvency or dishonesty of the man at the other end, or a storm at sea or a pirate's raid might spell ruin—these colonials who had set the pattern of their society and stood at its head would be quick to sense the first chill of any ill wind blowing from London. Any threat to their position in colonial society, to their pocketbooks, or to their political authority within the colony was sure to meet with their immediate resistance. The seat of this resistance would be their legislative assemblies. The basis of resistance would be rights held by the laws of God and Nature, and embodied in the British constitution, and rights won and confirmed by long usage. Their political assumptions would enable them to recognize any encroachment on their freedom of action for what it was; a common political vocabulary would enable them to translate their opposition into something their fellow colonists would understand and support. Any move by Britain tending to reduce the scope of colonial autonomy would become an attack on individual liberty; to oppose the move would be to champion the cause of human freedom against the threat of tyranny.

In 1763-1764 George Grenville hit colonial pocketbooks by tightening the supervision of colonial trade and further restricting use of paper money. The next year with the passage of the Stamp Act, Parliament launched what the colonial leaders conceived to be a fatal attack on their position and their authority. It was then that Britons and Americans began to comprehend what one hundred and fifty years in America had done to the Europeans who had moved to its shores.

Chapter IX

Notes on Sources

Anyone picking up this little volume may well ask why we should have yet another quick survey of early American history. If he goes one step further and reads the book he will find no ready answer to his question. His time will not have been wasted, however, if the book teaches him anything worth his knowing: makes him see a connection he has not seen, raises problems he has not considered, or provides him with useful insights or information. And his time will have been well spent if the book also prompts him to partake of the feast of which it is little more than a warmed-over serving.

To make the book a point of departure for a foray into the writings on the colonial origins of American society and its institutions one has only to check out some of the things the author has dealt with. It is always useful to take a look at any historian's sources, and in a work of this sort such inquisitions should lead directly to the best studies on any number of important topics relating to early American history.

The account in Chapter III of the colonization of Virginia is a case in point. It is based largely on W. Frank Craven's treatment of the subject in his volume on the southern colonies in the seventeenth century, which is a subtle and wise analysis both of the Jamestown experience and of the colonization process in general. Although many other things have been written about seventeenth-century Virginia, Professor Craven's work, taken together with two articles—one by Sister Joan de Lourdes Leonard and another by Bernard Bailyn—and the first volume of a two-volume work by Richard L. Morton, are sufficient not only to provide a fair overview of what happened between the landing at Jamestown and the arrival of Governor Francis Nicholson in 1690 but also to reveal where this author got most of his ideas and information on the subject.

Far more has been written about Massachusetts in the seventeenth century than about early Virginia. Many of the complexities and subtleties of the Puritan experiment in Massachusetts can be most readily got at in the writings of such contemporary scholars as Edmund S. Morgan, Bernard Bailyn, and Darrett B. Rutman. Rutman's reconstruction of the process by which the early arrivals in Massachusetts established communities around the shores of Massachusetts Bay, Morgan's illumination of the politics of Puritan Massachusetts in the 1630s through the life of John Winthrop, and Bailyn's investigation of the gradual emergence of the New England merchants as the dominant element in Massachusetts society and politics, are the superior stuff out of which the standard view of early Massachusetts is now formed.

The first half of the eighteenth century has not held the same fascination for historians as have the early days of colonization that preceded it or the ensuing Revolution. Still, there is a respectable body of work dealing with the impact of growth upon colonial society and institutions after 1700. One has only to look at the work of Jack Greene on legislative politics, Timothy Smith or Sidney Mead on the role of organized religion, Winthrop Jordan on slavery, Bailyn and Lawrence Cremin on education, Carl Bridenbaugh on cities, or Richard Pares on trade, to be assured that what has been called the most neglected period of American history has received the attention of distinguished historians.

When all is said and done, however, perhaps the best way to pursue a course of reading in colonial history is to follow one's nose, to let one thing lead to another. A perusal of Rutman's book just cited should reveal the merits, or the efficacy at least, of proceeding in this way. Dozens of topics worth exploring suggest themselves as one reads his book on the town of Boston; and the titles of scores of books and articles dealing with these topics appear in his footnotes and bibliography, offering further enlightenment on Anne Hutchinson, Puritan theology, the founding of Harvard College, the meaning of freemanship, early Massachusetts law, the ministry of John Cotton, the Puritan family, and so on. The literature devoted to the history of colonial America has become so extensive and is generally of so high a quality that one could move almost at random from book to book to article for months on end with pleasure and profit and without ever traversing the same ground.

It will not do to leave it at this, however. As anyone who has read this volume knows, the author has concentrated upon Virginia and Massachusetts to the neglect of England's other mainland colonies, and upon the emergence and growth of institutions with relatively little being said about how people lived from day to day in colonial America. It therefore seems appropriate to direct the reader without further ado to a few easily accessible and readable books which deal with things hardly touched upon here.

Any general interest in another colony besides Virginia or Massachusetts is easily met, whether it be New York or Georgia, New Hampshire or Maryland. For each colony there are one or more excellent studies of one sort or another which deal specifically with some aspect or period of that colony's history. Although one could hardly do better than to begin with some of the older works like those of Frederick Tolles on Quaker Pennsylvania or John Pomfret on East Jersey and West Jersey, there are several rather recent studies by young scholars which should not be overlooked. Among the best of these are Richard Bushman's investigation of social change and adjustment in eighteenth-century Connecticut, Stanley Katz's detailed account of factional politics in New York during the decades of the 1730s and 1740s, Gary Nash's suggestive study of political turbulence and political precocity in early Pennsylvania, and a straightforward but comprehensive political history of colonial South Carolina before 1750 by Eugene Sirmans. Each of these monographs in its own way looks forward to the great Revolution of the 1770s; in fact, most of the writings about colonial America reflect—both in direction of research and in the emphasis of interpretation—something of our shifting views about the meaning of 1776 and 1789.

Some of the more interesting work done in early American history in the 1960s dealt with a geographic unit smaller than the colony: the New England town. Demographic studies of seventeenth-century Andover and Dedham in Massachusetts-Bay Colony and of Plymouth, by Philip Greven, Kenneth Lockridge, and John Demos respectively, attracted particular notice. Their findings, first reported in articles and subsequently in book-length studies, brought into question several long-held assumptions about family life and social relations in seventeenth-century America. If, as Chapter I of this book argues, historians of early America tend to be interested either in tracing out European influences upon New World developments on the one hand or in searching for traits and institutions which owe relatively little to America's European heritage on the other, these monographs on New England towns if paired with the demographic studies of localities in seventeenth-century France and England, which served as models for the New England ones, suggest that certain things generally considered to be peculiarly American are more or less characteristic of society in the West at the time.

Among historians of both tendencies there are those who are less interested in studying a given time and place than in exploring some general trait or aspect of life in early America: law, architecture, trade, slavery, war, religion, the frontier, education, arts and letters, manners and customs. But no aspect of colonial America has received more attention from historians than the many facets of Puritanism. And for good reason. Some understanding of Puritan ideas and assumptions is necessary for an appreciation of certain basic truths about the American experience, colonial or national. Edmund Morgan's lucid essays on the Halfway Covenant entitled *Visible Saints: The History of a Puritan Idea* and Perry Miller's book of essays, *Errand into the Wilderness*, taken together provide the best introduction to Puritan thought. Having made the plunge, some will go on to read Miller's larger works, including his two volumes on the New England mind in the seventeenth and eighteenth centuries, Robert Middlekauff's new intellectual biography of three generations of Mathers, Samuel Eliot Morison's *The Puritan Pronaos,* or any one of dozens of other books and articles.

The truth is that a fair portion of the works devoted to social or cultural developments in colonial New England of any sort whatever are cast to a considerable extent in terms of the working out of Puritan ideas. A few cases more or less in point, all well worth reading, are George Haskins' monograph on law and authority in early Massachusetts, Middlekauff's study of schooling in eighteenth-century New England, and Alden Vaughan's book on warfare between the Indians and the Puritans on the New England frontier.

On the other hand, historians of the intellectual and cultural life of early America have not been bound solely to New England or concerned only with our Puritan heritage, although at times this would seem to be the case. A prime example of the social and cultural historian working mostly in areas outside New England is Carl Bridenbaugh. His writings on Philadelphia and Philadelphians in particular help correct any mistaken impression that before the era of the American Revolution the life of the mind did not exist to the south and west of the Hudson River.

The masterwork on the creation and functioning of the old British Empire remains the four-volume history by Charles Andrews: *The Colonial Period of American History.* The most provocative general treatment of the colonial period is the first volume of Daniel Boorstin's *The Americans.* The most authoritative and best balanced overview of the period is provided in Clarence Ver Steeg's *The Formative Years, 1607-1763.* And the best place I know to find the titles of useful books about every aspect of early American history is in the selected bibliography prepared by the Institute of Early American History and Culture: *Books about Early America* (Williamsburg, 1970).

The titles listed below are the works that have been referred to in this chapter. Asterisks indicate the volume is available in paperback.

Andrews, Charles M. *The Colonial Period of American History,* 4 vols. (New Haven, 1934-1938).*

Bailyn, Bernard. *Education in the Forming of American Society . . .* (Chapel Hill, 1960).*

——*The New England Merchants in the Seventeenth Century* (Cambridge, Mass., 1955).*

——"Politics and Social Structure in Virginia," in James M. Smith, ed., *Seventeenth-Century America: Essays in Colonial History* (Chapel Hill, 1959), 90-115.*

Battis, Emery. *Saints and Sectaries: Anne Hutchinson and the Antinomian Controversy in Massachusetts Bay Colony* (Chapel Hill, 1962).

Boorstin, Daniel J. *The Americans: The Colonial Experience* (New York, 1958).*

Bridenbaugh, Carl and Jessica. *Rebels and Gentlemen: Philadelphia in the Age of Franklin* (New York, 1942).*

Bridenbaugh, Carl. *Cities in the Wilderness: The First Century of Urban Life in America, 1625-1742* (New York, 1938).*

——*Cities in Revolt: Urban Life in America, 1743-1776* (New York, 1955).*

——*Myths and Realities: Societies of the Colonial South* (Baton Rouge, 1952).*

Bushman, Richard L. *From Puritan to Yankee: Character and the Social Order in Connecticut, 1690-1765* (Cambridge, Mass., 1967).*

Craven, Wesley Frank. *The Southern Colonies in the Seventeenth Century, 1607-1689* (Baton Rouge, 1949).*

Greene, Jack P. *The Quest for Power: The Lower Houses of Assembly in the Southern Royal Colonies, 1689-1776* (Chapel Hill, 1963).

Hall, Michael G. *Edward Randolph and the American Colonies, 1676-1703 (Chapel Hill, 1960).* *

Haskins, George Lee. *Law and Authority in Early Massachusetts: A Study in Tradition and Design* (New York, 1960).

Jordan, Winthrop D. *White Over Black: American Attitudes Toward the Negro, 1550-1812* (Chapel Hill, 1968).*

Katz, Stanley N. *Newcastle's New York: Anglo-American Politics, 1732-1753* (Cambridge, Mass., 1968).

Leonard, Sister Joan de Lourdes. "Operation Checkmate: The Birth and Death of a Virginia Blueprint for Progress." *William and Mary Quarterly,* 3rd Ser., XXXIV (Jan. 1967), 44-74.

Mead, Sidney E. *The Lively Experiment: The Shaping of Christianity in America* (New York, 1963).

Middlekauff, Robert. *Ancients and Axioms: Secondary Education in Eighteenth-Century New England* (New Haven, 1963).

——*The Mathers: Three Generations of Puritan Intellectuals, 1596-1728* (New York, 1971).

Miller, Perry. *Errand into the Wilderness* (Cambridge, Mass., 1956).*

——*The New England Mind: The Seventeenth Century* (New York, 1939).*

——*The New England Mind: From Colony to Province* (Cambridge, Mass., 1953).*

Morgan, Edmund S. *The Puritan Dilemma: The Story of John Winthrop* (Boston, 1958).*

——*Visible Saints: The History of a Puritan Idea* (New York, 1963).*

Morison, Samuel Eliot. *The Founding of Harvard College* (Cambridge, Mass., 1935).

——*The Puritan Pronaos* (New York, 1936). Republished as *The Intellectual Life of Colonial New England* (1956).*

Morton, Richard L. *Colonial Virginia,* 2 vols. (Chapel Hill, 1960).

Nash, Gary B. *Quakers and Politics: Pennsylvania, 1681-1726* (Princeton, 1968).

Pares, Richard. *Yankees and Creoles: The Trade Between North America and the West Indies before the American Revolution* (Cambridge, Mass., 1965).

Pomfret, John E. *The Province of East New Jersey, 1609-1702: The Rebellious Proprietary* (Princeton, 1962).

——*The Province of West New Jersey, 1609-1702: A History of the Origins of an American Colony* (Princeton, 1956).

Rutman, Darrett B. *Winthrop's Boston: Portrait of a Puritan Town, 1630-1649* (Chapel Hill, 1965).*

Sirmans, M. Eugene. *Colonial South Carolina: A Political History, 1663-1763* (Chapel Hill, 1966).

Smith, Timothy L. "Congregation, State and Denomination: The Forming of the American Religious Structure." *William and Mary Quarterly,* 3rd Ser., XXXV (April 1968), 155-176.

Sydnor, Charles S. *Gentlemen Freeholders: Political Practices in Washington's Virginia* (Chapel Hill, 1952). Republished as *American Revolutionaries in the Making . . .* (1962).*

Tolles, Frederick B. *James Logan and the Culture of Provincial America* (Boston, 1957).

——*Meetinghouse and Counting House: The Quaker Merchants of Colonial Philadelphia, 1682-1763* (Chapel Hill, 1948).*

Vaughan, Alden T. *The New England Frontier: Puritans and Indians, 1620-1675* (Boston, 1965).*

Ver Steeg, Clarence L. *The Formative Years, 1607-1763* (New York, 1964).

Ziff, Larzer. *The Career of John Cotton: Puritanism and the American Experience* (Princeton, 1962).

Index